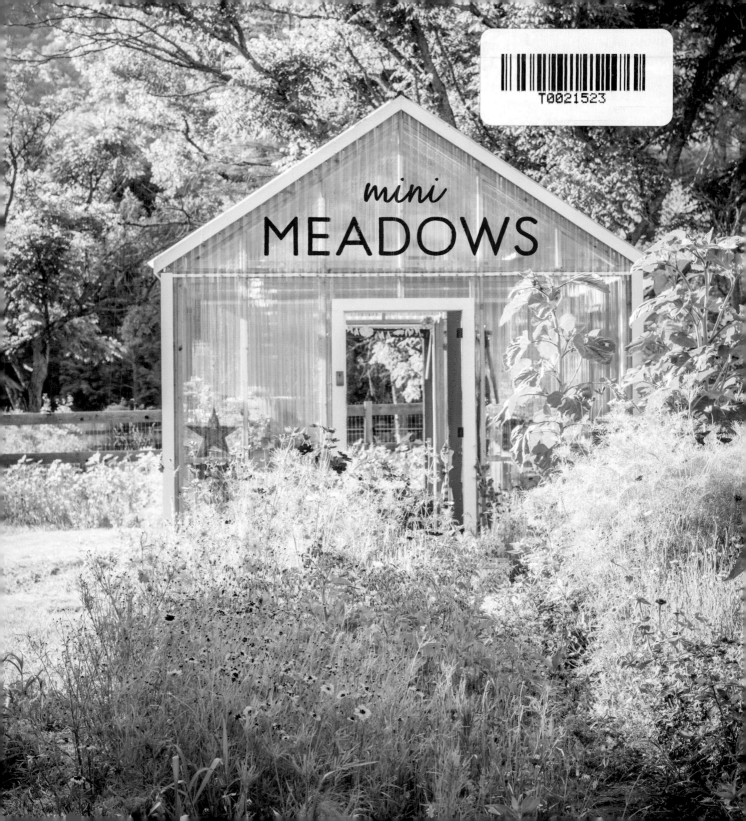

mini
MEADOWS

mini MEADOWS

Grow a Little Patch *of* Colorful Flowers *Anywhere* around Your Yard

BY MIKE LIZOTTE

Photography by Rob Cardillo

Storey Publishing

The mission of Storey Publishing is to serve our customers by publishing practical information that encourages personal independence in harmony with the environment.

Edited by Carleen Madigan
Art direction and book design by Michaela Jebb
Text production by Erin Dawson
Indexed by Nancy D. Wood

Cover photography by © Rob Cardillo, front, back t.r. & b.l.; Mars Vilaubi, back t.l.; © Friedrich Strauss/GAP Photos, back b.r.; © emer1940/iStock.com, spine 2nd from b.; © joloei/iStock.com, spine 2nd from t.; © jumnong/iStock.com, spine t.; © khudoliy/iStock.com, spine 3rd from b.; © Snowbelle/Shutterstock, spine 3rd from t.; © Topaz777/iStock.com, spine b.; © VIDOK/iStock.com, spine 3rd from b.

Interior photography by © Rob Cardillo, with designs by Chanticleer, 20 r., 95 b.r.; Jonathan Alderson, 102, 118; Larry Weaner, 96; Northcreek Nurseries, 58

Additional photography credits on page 141

Text © 2019 by Michael Lizotte

Storey Publishing
210 MASS MoCA Way
North Adams, MA 01247
storey.com

Storey Publishing is an imprint of Workman Publishing, a division of Hachette Book Group, Inc., 1290 Avenue of the Americas, New York, NY 10104

ISBNs: 9781612128351 (Paperback);
        9781612128368 (eBook)

Printed in China by Toppan Leefun Ltd. on paper from responsible sources
10 9 8 7 6 5 4 3 2

Library of Congress Cataloging-in-Publication Data on File

Storey books are available at special discounts when purchased in bulk for premiums and sales promotions as well as for fund-raising or educational use. Special editions or book excerpts can also be created to specification. For details, please send an email to special.markets@hbgusa.com.

CONTENTS

Preface
MY LIFE IN MEADOWS

It all started when I was 14 years old. A local seed company had a large ship-
ment arriving, and a high school friend of mine who worked there recruited
me to help out. Well, I must of have done something right, because they
asked me to come back. I started mowing the display gardens and doing
other outdoor maintenance on a regular basis. Shortly after that, I started
packing seed on the weekends. And that's where my lifelong journey in
meadow gardening began.

I must admit that I wasn't really into plants as a teenager. But as I began
packing seed, I became familiar with hundreds of different flowers. You could
lay the seeds of 50 different varieties on a table, and I could identify every
single one. What I couldn't tell you though, was what the flower looked like.
So, unlike most people who learn about plants by gardening or looking at
pictures of flowers, I learned the seed first and the plant and flower second.
In the years that followed, I started working behind the counter at the company's retail location. I continued to learn about different plants, spending
time in our display gardens and reading books on meadow gardening by
authors such as Jim Wilson, Laura C. Martin, and Rick Imes.

As an 18-year-old, I got my fair share of doubter looks when people came
to the retail counter to ask for meadow gardening advice. I used these looks
as motivation to learn everything I could about the plants and how to grow
them, so that I could prove to customers that I really did know what I was
talking about.

It was also around this time that my nickname, "the Seed Man," came to be. As customers entered the seed shop, they'd see me behind the counter and say, "You must be the Seed Man." I loved it! I had T-shirts made with THE SEED MAN printed on the back in big letters.

Over the years, I developed relationships with customers from across the country. Many of them would come into the shop or call to tell me how their meadows were progressing and how much they were enjoying it. Knowing that I had helped them was rewarding and such a source of satisfaction for me. By the time I was 21 and out of college, I had been fortunate enough to engage with tens of thousands of enthusiastic gardeners.

In my job at the seed company, I wasn't just learning about plants and wildflowers. I was very much inspired by the owners of the company, Ray and Chy Allen, and their work ethic. They were the first ones in the office and the last ones to leave. They were so passionate about flowers and about their customers! They always smiled and treated everyone with the utmost respect. Even when an employee made a mistake, they never dwelled on it; rather, they encouraged people and helped them succeed. Their leadership, drive, and passion for the business motivated me. I wouldn't be where I am now without their inspiration.

In 2009 my business partner, Ethan, and I were fortunate enough to be able to take over the seed business from Ray and Chy. As a business owner, my responsibilities have changed through the years, but there's not much I enjoy more than talking to someone about planting meadows. I love sharing my knowledge and getting people excited about gardening! I hope I can inspire you to plant a meadow and experience the same joy and passion I've shared with people across the country for more than 27 years.

Mike Lizotte

IX

You've Got the Perfect Spot for a Meadow

What do you think of when you hear the word "meadow"? A wild, grassy expanse where birds nest and prairie dogs scurry? A hayfield? The dictionary defines a meadow as "land that is covered or mostly covered with grass." Maybe, in your vision, there are a few wildflowers blooming among the grasses.

My definition of a meadow is slightly different. First off, I think of it as a place that isn't necessarily dominated by grasses but that includes all kinds of plants, both native and not, perennial and annual. A beautiful meadow should have flowers blooming from spring through the early frosts of fall. It most likely has a loose, naturalistic style and shouldn't be overly manicured. And because these plants typically offer food and habitat for insects and birds, there are butterflies and other pollinators flying around.

For the purposes of this book, a meadow can be any size — it can be in a planter box on your rooftop or it can occupy a few thousand square feet on the back edge of your property. It doesn't need to be big! The most important thing is to think of a meadow as a kind of garden that's loose and informal and that doesn't take a lot of time to maintain. It shouldn't be a burden. Allow it to develop and mature on its own, year after year, while you learn from and enjoy the process as you go.

For the past 25 years, I've been fortunate to have spoken and worked with gardeners of all levels, all over the world, walking them through the process of creating the meadow of their dreams. The fun and exciting part for me is that each meadow planting is unique and different — from a 300-acre commercial planting in Alabama to a rooftop garden in Dallas. Meadows can be defined in many ways, and each one carries its own unique stamp that reflects the aesthetics of the gardener as well as the conditions of the site; that's one of the great things about them.

In this book, I'm going to walk you through how to create your own meadow, step by step. Whether you have 10,000 square feet or 10, my instructions and planting tips will put you on the path to succeed and help you create a meadow that you can enjoy year after year. I'll also give you basic plant recommendations and hopefully leave you with ideas and tips to inspire you to create your very own mini meadow.

In a neighborhood of manicured lawns and clipped hedges, your yard can be a haven for pollinators.

WHY PLANT *a* MEADOW?

I can't tell you how many times people call me after their first and second years with their meadow, raving about how much they've enjoyed it. They love the endless color, the ever-changing look, and the constant buzzing of pollinators. They also love not having to mow every week! Meadows require little maintenance once established and provide enjoyment for years to come. Here are just a few more reasons why you should consider converting part of your lawn into a beautiful meadow.

CULTIVATE BEAUTY

Who doesn't love flowers? Regardless of how big or small an area you may have, meadow gardening can bring color to your yard, year after year. The best part is that with a little planning, it's much easier than you might think. Want quick color? Incorporate some annuals into your meadow. If you want more lasting color, perennials are the perfect choice! You have hundreds of colors, heights, and sizes to choose from, allowing you to create a meadow that is specific to your growing area and conditions (see page 123). You'll be able to enjoy the meadow from afar while having fresh-cut flowers on your dining table all summer.

ENGAGE KIDS

There's nothing more satisfying to me than spending the summer exploring flower meadows with my six-year-old daughter, Sadie. Each year we sit down and plan our meadows, adding new flowers and Sadie's favorite colors or shapes. She also started a journal to identify all the different critters that visit each year. Whether you are sowing seeds or learning about pollinators, you'll find that meadow gardening is a great way to get kids involved in gardening at an early age. And thanks to the ever-changing blooms and colors, children will stay engaged. And I'm always surprised how quickly they absorb and understand the miniature world of the meadow.

"Why try to explain miracles to your kids when you can just have them plant a garden?"

Richard Brault

Guessing Bloom Time with Kids

My daughter and I like to play a game called "When will it bloom?" We go out to the meadow and identify different plants in bud, then try to guess how many days it will take the flower to open. It's a great way for both kids and adults to learn to identify flowers and figure out how long they take to bloom.

Guessing bloom time can also be a chance to learn how weather affects flowers. It's often surprising how bloom times can vary depending on the weather. In my own meadow, when we've had mild springs and hot summers, I've seen plants come into flower weeks earlier than in previous years. When we've had cold springs and damp summers, we usually see flowers bloom a little later.

Meadow plants such as
borage provide pollinators
with nectar and pollen.

CONSERVE WATER

Did you know that landscape irrigation accounts for 9 billion gallons of water usage every day in the United States? The average American uses approximately 320 gallons of water a day, of which 30 percent is used on the lawn and gardening activities. That's a lot of H_2O! With proper planning, a meadow garden that includes drought-resistant and native varieties will help you cut back on watering and conserve thousands of gallons of water each year. Many meadow plant varieties require less moisture to thrive and can withstand longer periods of drought than varieties that you might find in a more formal garden setting.

HELP *the* POLLINATORS

Insects are critical to the pollination of crops that account for approximately 75 percent of food worldwide. In the United States, pollination plays a key role in producing crops such as almonds, apples, berries, and cucumbers — generating roughly 20 billion dollars' worth of food each year. And yet we are losing bees and other pollinators at concerning rates because of issues such as colony collapse disorder, pests and viruses, increased use of pesticides, and lack of genetic diversity. What better way to support pollinators than to create a meadow that includes nectar-rich meadow flowers, such as asters, butterfly weed, coneflower, joe-pye weed, zinnias, and cosmos?

ATTRACT BIRDS

A well-designed meadow will provide habitat and food for our winged friends. Flowers such as cosmos, daisies, and sunflowers produce seed that the birds will flock to for feeding. As the growing season winds down, the dead stalks and flower heads provide the perfect nesting material.

MOW LESS!

The U.S. Environmental Protection Agency estimates that more than 17 million gallons of gas are spilled each year by people fueling up lawn equipment. (Just so you know, that's more than the Exxon *Valdez* spill in Alaska.) The average gas lawnmower produces enough pollutants in one hour of use to equal 11 cars being driven for the same amount of time. When you replace your lawn with a beautiful meadow, you cut down on mowing and use (and spill!) less gas. Most meadow gardens are mowed only once or twice a year, which means you can spend more time enjoying your meadow and less time with the power equipment.

TACKLE HILLS *and* HELLSTRIPS

Do you have a hilly part of the yard that's a pain in the neck to mow every week? Or maybe a boggy area or a new septic field you'd like to plant over? How about beautifying that median or strip of grass along the sidewalk (also known as the "hellstrip")? Creating an eye-catching, low-maintenance, and tough-as-nails meadow is the perfect solution.

Most meadow gardens are mowed only once or twice a year, which means you can spend more time enjoying your meadow and less time with the power equipment.

a CUT-FLOWER MEADOW

Audrey planted up her walkway with a meadow mix designed to provide fresh-cut flowers all season long — a robust blend of annuals and perennials. There's nothing more satisfying than going out and cutting a fresh arrangement of flowers for the dinner table. A combination of annuals such as sunflowers, zinnias, cosmos, and cleomes can provide big color and beautiful cut flowers in year one. Perennials such as purple coneflower, bee balm, blanketflower, and blazing star will start bursting with flowers in the second year. To avoid creating bare spots in the meadow, it's best to avoid cutting too many flowers at a time. And adding grasses to a cut-flower meadow will contribute texture and beautiful contrast to any cut-flower bouquet.

Before

After

CHAPTER 1

Meadow Planning 101

Whether your meadow is big or small, it's important to set realistic expectations from the start, to avoid frustration and disappointment later on. After all, planting a meadow is much like planting any other kind of garden — good soil preparation and regular watering (especially early in the process, as the seeds are germinating) are very important.

To get the look you want, it's helpful if you identify the purpose, goal, or theme of your meadow planting. Let's say you're planning a wedding or other special event and you want a meadow as a backdrop for photography or to create some bouquets. The event is in the fall, and you want to plant this spring. You'll need to put in annuals, then — these will flower and complete their life cycle in one growing season. (Some popular annuals that you might already be familiar with are sunflowers, cosmos, zinnias, and marigolds.)

Or maybe you'd like to create a habitat to support pollinators. You're not in a rush, and you expect your meadow project to evolve over several years. There's no need for instant gratification in this scenario, so perennials — plants that come back year after year — can provide the perfect solution for creating a successful pollinator meadow. Knowing these details from the beginning will help you plan and better understand your meadow, how it may evolve, and the time and money it may take to achieve.

EVALUATE *Your* SITE

Now that you've done some thinking about what you want from your meadow, it's time to begin mapping out your plan of attack. There are a few keys to success that will apply to all planting scenarios, regardless of how big or small your meadow may be. What follows is a helpful meadow prep road map.

OBSERVE *and* TAKE NOTES

When I'm speaking with someone who wants to create a meadow, I usually recommend that we begin with a simple site analysis in the area they'd like to plant. You can learn a lot just by observing what's currently growing (or not growing) on your potential meadow site. Start by looking around and taking a few notes:

» Are there plants currently growing in the area you want to develop? How difficult will it be to remove them to prepare the site for your meadow?

» Are there any spots that are bare or have uneven growth? This could be an indicator of poor soil or lack of fertility; adding some compost will encourage better growth.

» Is the area boggy, or does it tend to be drier than other spots on your property? You'll want to select a plant mix that's suited to the site.

Fortunately, most meadow garden plants tend to be both hardy and tolerant of a range of soil conditions, so chances are you won't have to worry about getting a soil test or bringing in soil to establish your meadow. On pages 18 and 19, we'll learn more about how to evaluate your soil.

When choosing your meadow site, look to the landscape for clues on where to plant. For example, the patchy spots in part of this lawn indicate that there may be too much shade (or too little fertility) to successfully grow a meadow.

15

16

LET *the* SUN SHINE

Most meadow plant varieties are going to want some sun, so take note of how many hours a day the sun shines on your potential planting area. In addition, it's helpful to identify any trees that are on or near your site and where they cast their shade. Don't let a little shade get you down, though! In most cases, if the area receives five or six hours of direct sun a day, the meadow will thrive. And if you're getting only two or three hours of direct sun, or if the site only gets filtered sunlight, you should seek out varieties that grow well in partial shade. There are plenty of options to choose from, so don't feel discouraged if you don't have full sun.

Eight Plants for Partial Shade

If you're worried that you don't have enough sun to be successful with a meadow, try a few of these plants:

Wild columbine (*Aquilegia vulgaris*)

Johnny jump-up (*Viola cornuta*)

Forget-me-not (*Myosotis sylvatica*)

Siberian wallflower (*Cheiranthus allionii*)

Foxglove (*Digitalis purpurea*)

Drummond phlox (*Phlox drummondii*)

Sweet pea (*Lathyrus odoratus*)

Cornflower or bachelor's button (*Centaurea cyanus*)

Even though most meadow plants are tough as nails, it's still a good idea to have a basic idea of what your soil conditions are, so that you can make adjustments as needed and so that you can choose the right seed mix for your site. A simple, fast, and free way to learn about your soil is to simply observe what's currently growing in your potential planting area. If the area supports lush growth of grasses and other plants, the soil is probably just fine for planting a meadow. If the area has spotty growth with lots of bare spots, or if you've tried to plant there in the past with little success, you'll probably have to amend the soil.

Meadow plants might be tough, but they aren't miracle workers; they still need nutrients from the soil to thrive and soil that isn't compacted. Sometimes adding compost or other organic matter is all that's needed, especially if you've planted seeds or plants in the past with mixed results (such as if the plants have lots of foliage but not many flowers, or if the plants don't grow quickly enough to outcompete the weeds). A soil test would be helpful for identifying how to best address the situation.

For a detailed analysis of your soil, take a soil sample and send it to your local branch of the Cooperative Extension Service (see Resources, page 134). There is usually a small fee, but the analysis will give you precise information about your soil composition and any deficiencies it might have.

The Importance of Soil Structure

There is one important aspect of your soil you can determine by simple observation: what type of soil you have. The three most common types are sandy, clay, or loamy. Knowing which of these components is most prevalent in your soil will help you choose plants for your particular conditions. For example, there are plants that actually thrive in clay soil and help break up compacted areas, for the benefit of other plants. (See page 20 for a list of these plants.)

Sandy. Sandy soil is very well drained, contains large particles, and is typically low in nutrients. It's usually very easy to work with when preparing a meadow. Plants that thrive in well-drained sites and can tolerate a lack of moisture are perfect for planting in sandy soil.

Clay. Clay soil does not drain quickly but is typically full of nutrients. It contains very small soil particles that stick together and is often compacted and challenging to work with. Choosing the rights plants is key, but you may also want to add organic matter to lighten the soil. If you have very heavy clay soil and you're going to use a tiller to prepare the area and mix in compost, it may take a few tillings for you to break up the soil. I recommend doing a test run to make sure your tiller can handle the density of the clay.

Loamy. Some might say a loamy soil is ideal, as it contains a nice balance of clay, sand, and organic matter. It usually the easiest to work, and most anything will grow in it. If you find yourself with a loamy soil, consider yourself lucky, as it's hard to come by in a natural setting. Most of us will be starting with a sandy or clay "base" and may have to amend by adding organic matter or compost to attain loamy conditions.

Butterfly weed
Asclepias tuberosa

Plains coreopsis
Coreopsis tinctoria

Purple coneflower
Echinacea purpurea

Eight Clay-Busting Plants

Some plants actually thrive in clay and can help break it down over time. A few of these claybusters are:

Purple milkweed (*Asclepias purpurascens*)

Butterfly weed (*Asclepias tuberosa*)

Plains coreopsis (*Coreopsis tinctoria*)

Purple coneflower (*Echinacea purpurea*)

Rough blazing star (*Liatris aspera*)

Black-eyed Susan (*Rudbeckia hirta*)

Mealycup sage (*Salvia farinacea*)

African marigold (*Tagetes erecta*)

The Ins and Outs of Fertilizer

Because most meadow plants are very hardy and can tolerate a range of growing conditions, you probably won't need additional fertilizer. If you decide you'd like to add fertilizer to give your plants a boost, here are a few tips to keep in mind:

Learn to read the labels. There are many different types of fertilizer, but they all usually include three numbers, separated by dashes — such as 10-10-10. These represent the three main nutrients plants need to survive: nitrogen (N), phosphorus (P), and potassium (K). The number is the percentage of each nutrient included. Nitrogen is primarily responsible for promoting vigorous green growth in plants. Phosphorus is critical in supporting healthy root growth and plays a role in flower production as well. Potassium supports the growth of the plants, from leaves to roots and flower production. It plays a key role in plant photosynthesis and respiration, activating enzymes that help the plant's overall growth and water use, which is critical in times of drought. Potassium also aids in cell production that strengthens and protects the plant from disease, heat, cold, and other extreme conditions.

Start with just a little. Regardless of the type of fertilizer you choose, it's important to remember that more isn't better. Adding fertilizer when it's not necessary can actually work against you, by making the soil just as inviting for weeds and grass as for your meadow plants. If you must add fertilizer, always read the instructions and start with a light application at first to see how the plants respond.

Kids can definitely help with watering, but you'll probably also want to use a sprinkler, so make sure your meadow isn't located too far from a hose bib. Newly sown meadows need frequent, deep watering when they're getting established.

PLAN *for* WATERING

Even though meadow plants can be remarkably drought tolerant once they're established, they benefit from regular watering early on — especially when the seeds are just starting to germinate. If seedlings don't have enough water at this stage, they may not be able to outcompete the weed seeds in the surrounding soil (which are better adapted to growing without much water). If you're able to set a sprinkler in your newly seeded patch, or if you schedule your planting to occur just before a stretch of rainy weather, you'll give your meadow a good start in life.

Decide how much you're willing to water after the meadow is established and make a plan for watering based on that. If you don't want to water your meadow, consider selecting varieties that can grow with just the amount of rainfall your region receives. If you'd prefer to (or must) water, make sure to consider how far away your water source will be. This is important not only for a meadow in the ground but also for one in a raised bed or planter. How far will you have to carry your watering can or drag a hose?

Survival of the Fittest

What happens when you forget to water? One of our colleagues found out when she went away for a long weekend and the weather turned too hot and dry for her freshly germinated meadow. She watered and watered when she returned, but it was too late — most of the seedlings had died. She thought all was lost until she saw tiny sprouts of California poppy and marigold coming up. Although she didn't end up with the lush, multicolored meadow she was hoping for, she did have a lovely patch of orange flowers. And she learned a new appreciation for the most drought-tolerant plants in the meadow mix.

KNOW YOUR ZONE *and* REGION

Another important piece of gardening information to know is your USDA Hardiness Zone. These zones are based on the average minimum temperature in a given area, and they were created as a way to help consumers select plants that will survive the winter. Use the USDA Hardiness Zone Map (see page 135) to find your zone. When sourcing your plants, make sure they're all labeled with the proper growing zone.

This mini meadow is a lush oasis in the dry Colorado landscape that surrounds it.

The good news is that a lot of plants do well in many different zones. Also keep in mind that every zone has microclimates (areas that are cooler or warmer than the surrounding region). Because of that, you may well be able to grow plants that are not considered hardy for your area. You will learn over time how much wiggle room you have when selecting plants for your zone.

In some cases, meadow seed mixtures are marketed for particular regions rather than for zones. The reason for this is that most seed mixes contain a blend of flowering plants and/or grasses that can thrive in multiple zones. Also, gardeners (both novice and experienced) sometimes relate to the idea of regions a little more easily than to zones. See page 123 for some of my meadow mix recommendations for different regions.

KNOW PLANT LIFE CYCLES *for* BETTER PLANNING

Whether you're a Master Gardener or you're planning your first meadow, it's important to understand the life cycles of the plants you'll be growing. This is key, both so that you have a sense of what to expect and so that you can create a successful planting plan. A good meadow mix should be properly marked with the species and life cycle information of each type of seed in the mix. Any plant you purchase should have a tag that indicates whether it is an annual, perennial, or biennial.

PLANT ANNUALS *for* QUICK *and* EASY COLOR

An annual is a plant that completes its life cycle in one growing season. The seed is planted, grows, produces a flower, develops and drops seed, and then dies. You'll only see that flower again next year if it produces seeds that overwinter in the soil and sprout the following spring.

If you're looking for quick color in the first growing season, plan on including some annuals in your meadow. Listed or shown below are some you might be familiar with:

» Spiderflower (*Cleome hassleriana*)

» Plains coreopsis (*Coreopsis tinctoria*)

» Cosmos (*Cosmos bipinnatus*)

» Rocket larkspur (*Delphinium ajacis*)

» California poppy (*Eschscholzia californica*)

» Indian blanket (*Gaillardia pulchella*)

» Baby's breath (*Gypsophila elegans*)

» Rose mallow or tree mallow (*Lavatera trimestris*)

» Scarlet flax (*Linum grandiflorum* var. *rubrum*)

» Sweet alyssum (*Lobularia maritima*)

» Lemon mint (*Monarda citriodora*)

» California bluebell (*Phacelia campanularia*)

» French marigold (*Tagetes patula*)

» Strawflower (*Xerochrysum bracteatum*)

Sunflower
Helianthus annuus

Cornflower or bachelor's button
Centaurea cyanus

Zinnia
Zinnia species

Red poppy, Shirley poppy, or corn poppy
Papaver rhoeas

Calendula or pot marigold
Calendula officinalis

Love-in-a-mist
Nigella damascena

Crimson clover
Trifolium incarnatum

Lacy phacelia
Phacelia tanacetifolia

MEADOW PLANNING 101

PLANT PERENNIALS *for* LONG-LASTING COLOR

For lasting color that comes back for several years, include a blend of perennial plants in your meadow. A plant with a perennial life cycle may not flower during its first year of growth from seed. The plant will go dormant during the winter and in the second growing season will put on growth and begin to flower. It will then continue to bloom every season thereafter, until the end of its life span (most perennials live for at least a few years).

If you are purchasing perennial plants or plugs and you notice they already have top growth and even flowers, it's always a good idea to ask how old the plants are. This will help you set the proper expectations for your meadow and better understand when your new perennials might bear blossoms. Most perennials come into bloom in the second growing season, but there are a few perennials that can produce a flower from seed in the first season.

28

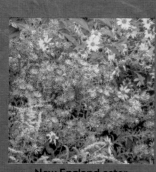

New England aster
Symphyotrichum novae-angliae

Butterfly weed
Asclepias tuberosa

Wild lupine
Lupinus perennis

Blue flax
Linum perenne

Anise hyssop
Agastache foeniculum

Pale purple coneflower
Echinacea pallida

Spotted joe-pye weed
Eupatorium maculatum

Eastern red columbine
Aquilegia canadensis

DON'T FORGET BIENNIALS

A biennial plant completes its life cycle in two growing seasons. It will put on top growth in the first growing season from seed, then go dormant through the winter months and return the second year with flowers. After the flowers fade, they'll produce seed and the plant will then die; the only way it will reappear in your garden is if it reseeds. Although using biennials can present a challenge for planning, you may well count them among your favorite plants and want to include them in your meadow.

Sweet William
Dianthus barbatus

Hooker's evening primrose
Oenothera elata subsp. *hookeri*

Stock
Matthiola incana

Hollyhock
Alcea rosea

Forget-me-not
Myosotis sylvatica

Foxglove
Digitalis purpurea

Standing cypress
Ipomopsis rubra

Prairie aster or tansy-leaf aster
Machaeranthera tanacetifolia

NATIVE PLANTS

The term "native" generally refers to plants that are indigenous to a particular place. For example, purple coneflower (*Echinacea purpurea*) is a popular perennial that is native in much of North America. Some people have taken the designation a step further and try to determine what is native to their state or region in particular.

There are good reasons to include native plants in your meadow. Natives play a critical role in sustaining the biodiversity of our ecosystems. Most North American native varieties are very hardy and can withstand a wide range of growing conditions. They also tend to require less water and less maintenance overall. And last (but certainly not least!), they play a key role in feeding and providing habitat for native insects, pollinators, and other wildlife.

Native plants can be a little more expensive, but because native species tend to be much hardier and outlast many nonnative species, the cost will even out in the long run. If you're purchasing native seeds, check to make sure the origin is clearly marked, and always ask for the germination and purity information.

Here are some natives you might want to try:

» Eastern red columbine (*Aquilegia canadensis*)
» Common milkweed (*Asclepias syriaca*)
» Lanceleaf coreopsis (*Coreopsis lanceolata*)
» Purple coneflower (*Echinacea purpurea*)
» Spotted joe-pye weed (*Eupatorium maculatum*)
» Prairie blazing star (*Liatris pycnostachya*)
» Cardinal flower (*Lobelia cardinalis*)
» Wild bergamot (*Monarda fistulosa*)
» New England aster (*Symphyotrichum novae-angliae*)
» Prairie ironweed (*Vernonia fasciculata*)

Sweet coneflower
(*Rudbeckia
subtomentosa*)
and New York
ironweed (*Vernonia
noveboracensis*)
make a stunning
native meadow.

It's okay to mix nonnative zinnias with native black-eyed Susans!

MIXING IN NONNATIVES

Are you drawn to the idea of an all-native meadow but are secretly a fan of zinnias and poppies? That's okay! Nonnative annuals provide beautiful color in the first growing season, and they'll help suppress unwanted annual weeds that might be tempted to move in while your native perennials are establishing themselves.

Too often, when you mention the term "nonnative," people mistakenly interpret it as "invasive," or otherwise doing harm to the environment. This couldn't be further from the truth. Simply because a nonnative plant doesn't come from your region, or even from North America, doesn't mean that it won't be beneficial for the environment. You can definitely create a meadow with a nice variety of both native and nonnative varieties. Annual species such as zinnias, cosmos, and cleomes are popular meadow varieties that will add big, quick color to any meadow planting. They can also be very helpful to pollinators and wildlife.

HOW MUCH SEED WILL *You* NEED?

When planning your meadow, it's important to calculate the square footage of the area you'd like to plant. Having this measurement makes it easier to determine the amount of seed or plants to buy. It will also help you decide how best to go about preparing your site.

WHAT IF IT'S *not* SQUARE?

A meadow can take on any number of different shapes and sizes, which makes it difficult to figure an exact size. Here's how to calculate the square footage of different shapes:

Square or rectangle. These are the easiest! Simply multiply length times width.

Circle. If you're dealing with a circle, multiply pi (3.1416) by the radius of the circle squared.

Triangle. If your meadow is shaped more like a triangle, you'll multiply the base times the height and then divide by two.

HOW MUCH SEED *per* SQUARE FOOT?

How much seed to plant will vary depending on the look you'd like to achieve. If you're planting pure seed (see page 50), the package might suggest ¼ pound to cover an area of 500 square feet. If you wanted an especially lush stand of plants, you may choose to plant ½ pound of seed — and that's fine. But don't go overboard and plant 2 pounds of seed in your 500 square feet; if you put too much seed down, the plants will compete, choking each other out and not growing well.

How to Calculate Square Footage

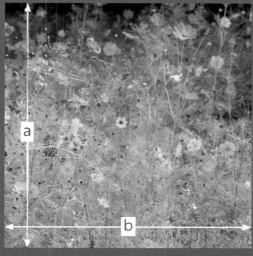

a × b

radius × 3.1416

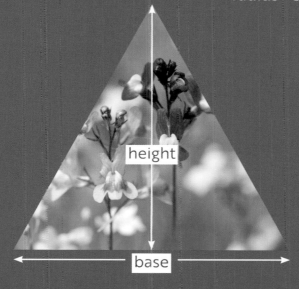

$$\frac{\text{base} \times \text{height}}{2}$$

CHAPTER 2

Digging In

Now that you've learned the basics of meadow planning, it's time to dig in! Thorough site preparation, even seeding, regular watering after planting, and careful observation are keys to starting a successful meadow. Determining when to sow your seed may also be a consideration, depending on where you live.

If there's one step in the process that warrants spending a little more time to get right, it's site preparation. Meadow plants may be tough once they become established, but they still need help getting started — that means preparing a bed of loose, friable soil and giving them regular moisture once they've germinated. Just imagine if you tried to sow seeds for lettuce or carrots or any other crop into a bed of weedy, compacted soil! A meadow is still a garden and, like any other garden, the better you prepare your soil, the better results you'll have — both this year and in the future.

GETTING RID
of WHAT'S THERE

Listen up! This is the most important step in creating a successful meadow. The more time you spend clearing the area of unwanted grasses and weeds, the better your meadow will be. Through my 25 years of helping gardeners across the country establish meadows, I've seen firsthand that this is the one step that can make or break your meadow planting.

TILLING *up* TURF

One of the most common ways to prepare your meadow area is using a tiller. Tillers can be very effective in breaking up the soil while grinding up existing weeds and grasses. They vary in size, from a small walk-behind tiller to a three-point-hitch tiller that attaches to the back of a tractor. They can be rented at most hardware stores without breaking the bank.

You'll only need to till deeply enough to break up the surface layer of plants and their roots. There's usually no need to go any deeper than 6 to 8 inches. In most cases, you'll want to go over the area two or three times, to grind up all the surface growth and break apart any large clods of soil. Rake up any remaining clods of turf. You'll be left with a nice, fluffy bed of soil that will help your seed germinate easily and evenly.

After tilling, rake up any remaining clods of turf and level out the soil to ensure even germination.

The Downside of Tilling

Any time you disturb the soil, you increase your chances of bringing dormant weed or grass seed to the surface, which isn't ideal when you're starting a meadow from scratch. Seeds can lay dormant in the soil for many years; when they're brought to the surface and exposed to sunlight and moisture, they germinate and create competition for your meadow seeds. When you're tilling your new garden, make sure you only go deep enough to break up the surface layer of growth. The deeper you till, the more seeds you'll bring up!

40

Smothering a future meadow site with black plastic for a full growing season is a great way to eliminate grass and other plants that might compete with your meadow seedlings.

SMOTHER IT!

If you have a small meadow — let's say a few hundred square feet or less — you can eliminate existing plants by smothering them. Before smothering, it's helpful to mow the area well, both to outline where the meadow will be and to speed the process of breaking down the plants.

Plastic sheeting. A layer of black plastic, secured around the edges with boards or landscape staples, will kill the growth underneath by cutting off sunlight and air. Some advance planning is required for this; the plastic should be left in place for at least a month. After you remove the plastic, you'll want to loosen the soil with a garden fork before you sow seed.

Cardboard or newspaper. Instead of plastic, you might choose to use cardboard or layers of newspaper to smother existing plants. This method can take anywhere from four months to a full growing season to be effective, so make sure you plan ahead.

Cover the entire area with three to five layers of newspaper or a single layer of cardboard, dampen it with a hose to help hold it in place, then spread 2 to 4 inches of mulch on top. Check every couple of months to see if any plants are still alive, and only proceed to planting when all the vegetation has been killed.

If you're planting from seed, rake all the mulch and any bits of undecomposed newspaper or cardboard off to the side of the garden before you sow. Once your seedlings have sprouted, you may choose to add the mulch back around the base of the plants to help suppress weeds.

If you're starting a meadow from plants, your job is a little easier: You can simply scrape back a bit of the mulch, dig your hole right through the newspaper or cardboard (if it hasn't broken down all the way), and plant. Once you've gotten your plants in the ground, you can then add the mulch back at the base of the plants.

ORGANIC SPRAYS

There are organic sprays that can be quite effective in killing off the weeds when preparing your meadow. Regular white vinegar can be effective when sprayed directly on certain weeds; even more potent is the horticultural grade of vinegar, which has a higher level of acetic acid. As with any potentially dangerous product, always follow the instructions on the label.

SYNTHETIC HERBICIDES

Several types of synthetic herbicide are readily available at most hardware stores and garden centers. Whether or not to use them is obviously up to you. Are they effective in killing vegetation? Yes. Are some of them linked to various cancers, declines in pollinator populations, and other harmful environmental ramifications? Yes. If you are thinking of applying any of these chemicals, do your homework first.

Preparing Soil for a Container Meadow

If you have a raised bed, window box, or other form of planter, preparation is also important but a lot easier. If you're planting in a raised bed, you could simply fill it with good, open-textured soil and a bit of compost. If you're planting in a container, make sure it has adequate drainage so that the plants' roots don't rot; containers should have enough holes in the bottom to allow water to flow through easily. Use potting mix rather than garden soil, which won't drain properly in a container.

A MINI MEADOW *in* *a* RAISED BED

A meadow can be defined many ways and can take on any number of shapes and sizes. Some of us don't have a lot of space to work with — a small raised bed or container is all we can manage. Fortunately, planting a meadow garden in a constructed space like this offers some advantages, including greater control over soil and site, as well as better accessibility.

Whether you purchase a raised-bed kit or get creative and make your own, here are a couple of tips that will help you along the way:

Choose the right-sized kit. There are hundreds of raised-bed kits, plus different-sized whiskey barrels and containers that would all work for creating your meadow. Don't get overwhelmed or think you need to pick the biggest one. Choose the size that will work for your space and your level of commitment (bigger = more maintenance!). When in doubt, start small.

Plan your plants to fit your small space. Don't think just because you have limited space that means you have limited selection. There are lots of plants that will do just fine in a raised bed (see page 108).

Be vigilant about watering. With small-space gardening, the soil tends to warm up quickly. This is great for the plants that are getting established in your meadow, but it also means the soil could dry up just as fast. Be aware, keep a close eye on your plantings, and water when the soil feels dry when you plunge a finger into it.

44

Spring is a good time to evaluate potential planting sites and identify any perennials you might need to work around or transplant to another location.

WHEN *to* PLANT

Both spring and fall can be good times to plant a meadow, depending on where you live and how much experience you have. For example, timing the fall planting of a cold-climate meadow can be a bit tricky. So if you're a northern gardener and this is your first time planting a meadow, I'd suggest sowing in spring. There's nothing wrong with a little experimenting, though, and you'll quickly learn which planting time is better for you.

PLANTING *in* SPRING

Spring is for gardening! We all get excited on that first mild day of spring after a long winter. We want to run outside and start planning our gardening projects for the season. Well, don't let that mild air fool you. The key to a successful spring planting is waiting until the *ground* temperature is warm enough, so that when you begin to plant, your seeds and plants will be ready to take off.

Wait for Warm Soil

Here's an analogy that I've been telling for years, which people seem to catch on to very quickly. I tell people that when you have that first warm day in spring, when it might get to be 65 or 75°F (18 or 24°C), you don't go jump into the Atlantic Ocean. Sure, the air temperature is nice, but the water is still 37°F (3°C). Ground temperature acts the same way: soil takes time to warm up in spring. So don't be fooled by warm *air* temperatures and plant too early. I can't tell you how many times the phone rings in early spring with customers panicking because they sowed their seed and nothing is happening after 20 days. We can usually trace their planting back to a warm day in March or April when the person planted, not realizing the ground temperatures were still very cold.

SEED MAN SAYS
Plant with Tomatoes

A good rule for planting your meadow in spring is to simply wait and sow seed at the same time you put your tomato plants out. That date will vary depending on where you live in the country, but it's usually a safe bet. It's always better to wait a little to plant than to sow too early.

What Happens if I Plant Too Early?

It's always best to be a little patient when planting in spring and let those ground temperatures warm up before you seed or plant your meadow. If you do make the mistake of planting too early, your seed will just sit on the cold ground until the soil warms up enough for germination to take place. If the seed actually does germinate and your garden is hit with a frost, your seedlings could be killed and you may have to sow more seed. If you've put plants in the ground, they'll act sluggish and may even wilt a bit until the ground warms up enough to stimulate the roots so they can begin growing. If a frost comes after they're in the ground, the plants should still be okay — they'll just need some time (and warmth!) to rebound.

FALL PLANTING MIGHT BE *for* YOU

Depending on where you live and what your growing season is like, fall may be a good time for planting. After all, in nature, seeds drop in fall, lay dormant through the winter months, and begin to germinate once the ground warms in spring. No matter where you live, fall is a great time to put plants in the ground; they won't be stressed from the summer heat, and the combination of warm soil and cool air means that roots will have time to settle in but the plants won't put energy into growing new foliage.

In Cold-Winter Regions

Fall seeding in regions that experience winters with freezing temperatures can be beneficial, allowing you get a jump-start on the following season and maximize your growing season. When planting your meadow from seed, you must wait until after you've had several frosts and the ground temperatures have cooled, so that the seed doesn't germinate. The seed will lay dormant through the winter months and begin to germinate once the ground warms in spring. I've seen fall-sown meadows bloom anywhere from 2 to 6 weeks earlier than spring-sown meadows.

If you're planting your meadow using container-grown plants or plugs, you'll want to get them in the ground up to a month before your first frost date. This will allow them enough time to set their roots in the warmer soil temperatures before the colder winter weather arrives.

In Warmer Regions

If you live in a region that experiences mild winters and hot summers, seeding or planting in fall works very well and gives your meadow the best chance to thrive. Cool temperatures and winter rains will help plants become established more easily and will get seeds off to a good start. A spring planting in warmer climates can be challenging and require constant watering, which isn't ideal.

If you live in a region that doesn't experience frosts or extended periods of cold weather, a fall planting can provide lasting color and flowers all through your winter, spring, and early-summer months. Once the extreme heat of summer arrives, your meadow will go dormant but will return come fall.

SEED MAN SAYS
Weed When Wet

Try to weed after a rainstorm, if you can. Pulling weeds when the soil is damp or wet is much easier. Also, if you do pull weeds, keep in mind it will create open pockets of soil. These are perfect for receiving more meadow seed, so be sure to have some extra on hand.

PLANTING *from* SEED

Now that you've prepared your meadow, it's time to sow. As with anything, you should always follow the instructions on your package of seed. Planting a package of 100 percent pure seed is different from planting a mix that is mostly filler.

When you open your seed packets, start by just noticing all the different seed sizes and shapes. They're amazing! Spend some time sifting them through your hands and observing. How many different varieties are you able to identify?

MIX SEED *with* SAND

When using 100 percent pure seed, you'll want to mix it with builders' or sandbox sand, at a ratio of five parts sand to one part seed, to make sure the seed is distributed evenly. If you were to spread your seed without adding a dispersing agent like sand, the lighter seed would fall in some areas and the heavier seed would fall in other areas. Mixing with sand also makes it easier to see exactly where the seed has been spread; the light color of the seed-and-sand mix is easy to identify as it lands on your dark soil. Be sure the sand is dry; otherwise, it won't mix evenly and will clog your spreader.

DISTRIBUTE *with a* SPREADER . . .

There are several ways you can go about sowing your seed, depending on the size of your meadow. A simple shoulder spreader can be very effective and a little faster than hand spreading. There are many handheld spreaders that will also do the trick. If you have a larger area that may have required a tractor to prepare, you can rent a steel seed spreader that fits on the back of the tractor.

Most spreaders allow you to adjust the settings based on the size of the seed you're sowing. I always recommend using the finest or smallest setting when spreading your meadow mix, though it may take a little experimenting with just sand to find the proper setting on your particular spreader.

... OR SPREAD *by* HAND

My preference is to forgo the spreader and do it by hand. I mix my seed and sand in a 5-gallon pail or wheelbarrow and then divide the mix into four equal parts. Then I fill a smaller bucket with a quarter of the seed-and-sand mix and walk around the meadow area, tossing handfuls of the mix with an underhand motion and a little flick of the wrist. After I've made one pass, I'll fill my bucket with another quarter of the mix and go over the entire area again in a different direction, then repeat until I've spread all the mix. By going over the entire area several times, I ensure a nice, evenly sown meadow.

Look for Quality Seed

When you're shopping for a meadow mix, you'll want the best-quality product you can find. Here's what to look for:

- A good meadow mix should have a balance of species that bloom all season long, with a nice blend of different heights and textures.

- Any product you buy should be 100 percent pure seed; many of the lower-quality products are mostly filler.

- The seed should be lab tested with germination and purity information provided on the label.

- The meadow mix should be from a reputable seed company, as they will be able to answer any questions you might have and provide additional information.

Comparison of quality seed mix vs. big box product

PRESS THE SEED *into the* SOIL

Once you've sown your seed, lightly press it into the soil. With smaller plantings, this can be done by simply laying a piece of cardboard over the planting area and walking over it. For larger meadow plantings, you can use a water-fill roller (which is usually available for rent if you don't own one). There's no need to add much water, as you don't need a lot of weight — just a little pressure to push the seeds down to ensure good seed-to-soil contact and better germination.

DO *Not* COVER

People often ask if they need to rake their seeds into the soil or cover them with soil. In most cases, the answer is no. Most wildflower or meadow mix seeds are small enough that if you rake them or cover them, some of them may end up planted too deep in the soil, and this would affect the germination rate of the mix.

The only time I recommend covering your seed is if you're planting on a slope. A light cover of chopped straw (not hay, as this may contain weed seeds) would help hold the seed. If the area is exposed to a lot of wind, you might also cover the seeds to keep them from being blown away. Be careful not to cover seeds too thickly; you still want water and sunlight to be able to penetrate. You also want your seedlings to be able to come up through the straw once they begin to germinate.

In the first day or two after seeding, don't be surprised if birds or other critters visit your soon-to-be meadow and munch on some seeds. Don't worry — they can snack on seeds without affecting the outcome of your meadow. When planting 100 percent pure seed, there could be between 200,000 and 300,000 seeds per pound (depending on your mix formulation). So if the birds eat a few, don't panic — there's plenty to go around.

WATER and WATCH for GERMINATION

Once you've planted your meadow, watch for the first signs of germination. Watering the area right after sowing will certainly help speed up the germination process. If you're not able or willing to water, you might consider scheduling your planting around a forecast period of rainy weather. In most cases, a high-quality meadow mix should germinate in 10 to 20 days. I've had seed sprout in as little as 5 days over a stretch of sunny weather when I kept the meadow well watered.

STORING SEEDS

If you have leftover seed after you've planted your meadow, you can store it for up to two years. Any container you choose — a mason jar or a plastic food container with a lid — should be securely sealed after it has been filled with seeds, so that no moisture can enter. Be sure to label the containers and store them in a cool, dry place. A refrigerator, kitchen cupboard, or a dry basement would work fine.

Buy a Blend or Mix Your Own?

Rather than purchase a premixed blend of seeds, you may choose to design your own mix or plant individual species from seed. This does take a little more understanding of the heights and bloom times of each flower, but it can be very rewarding and allows you to plant species exactly where you want them in your meadow.

STARTING *with* PLANTS *or* PLUGS

If you're looking for faster results, consider starting a meadow with both seed and plants. Most garden centers or nurseries offer a nice selection of both annuals and perennials in all sorts of colors, heights, and bloom times so you can plan your garden accordingly. Don't be afraid to ask for help at the garden center when choosing plants or mapping out your meadow garden. There are a lot of little details to consider, such as how tall and wide the plants will eventually be, as well as when they'll bloom. A good garden center or landscape designer can help put you on a path to succeed.

CHOOSING PLANTS

You will find meadow plants offered in a variety of different sizes. Bigger is not better when it comes to plants in pots, though. A 2- to 4-inch potted perennial will grow and become established more quickly than a plant that's in a 1-gallon or larger pot. After a year or two, the smaller plant will have become just as big as the larger plant, and most people wouldn't be able to tell the difference between the two. But where you *will* be able to tell is in your savings of money! The smaller plants are usually a fraction of the cost of the larger plants.

Once you've prepared your list of plants, I suggest that you make a planting plan, so that you know how many plants you'll need. Take into consideration how tall the plants will get and how much they'll spread. This will allow you to get a more accurate count on the quantity needed and calculate your costs properly.

GET PLANTING!

Having a planting plan will help you space plants appropriately, so they have room to grow. A common mistake people make is putting their plants too close together; the plants may look small in the beginning (especially if you're planting plugs), but in just a few short months, those plants will grow quickly.

Once you know the spread of your plants, you can mark the soil where you're going to dig your holes. Dig your holes so that they're twice the size of the pot that your plant is currently in; the extra space will encourage the roots to expand quickly in their new site. Tuck the plant into the hole, backfill with compost or topsoil, water it well, and cover the root zone (but not the foliage) with an organic mulch to help keep the soil moist.

It's not unusual to see some plants droop a little shortly after they go into the ground. This is natural as the plants adjust to their new environment and will usually last only 24 to 48 hours; then you should see them bounce right back.

A big benefit to using plugs or plants from containers is that most of the plants will be ready to flower that growing season. If you're putting in annuals, they could be ready to bloom in a matter of weeks. Perennials might also be ready to bloom quickly, depending on how old they were when you purchased them.

SEED MAN SAYS
Know Your Bloom Time

Know the bloom times of the plants and plugs you've selected, and don't choose too many that bloom at the same time as this could leave other times of the year with limited color. A landscape designer or nursery should be able to help you with this planning. Bloom time information should be found on all the plant tags as well.

Your MEADOW IS ALIVE!

As those first few weeks go by, continue to take notice of the weather, as this will play a big part in the development of your meadow. It's ideal to have some rain in the forecast or to water your meadow to stimulate growth during those first few weeks after sowing or planting. If it's been sunny and you've been watering or getting rain and things *still* seem slow to progress, it's a good time to troubleshoot.

TROUBLESHOOTING *Your* MEADOW

No germination at all. If a few weeks have passed and the area has been receiving lots of sun and regular moisture, yet the ground still looks pretty bare, this raises some concern. A high-quality meadow mix should germinate in 10 to 20 days with proper sun and moisture. If it's been 30 days and there's very little growth, the problem may be a lack of soil fertility. You might consider doing a soil test to help pinpoint the possible areas of concern.

It looks like there are just grasses and weeds growing. This may be the result of sowing seed too sparsely. Did you calculate the area or square footage properly to ensure you purchased the right amount of seed? If you sowed too little in relation to the actual size, this could allow weeds to gain the upper hand.

There's growth in some areas but not others. This suggests that the seeds weren't evenly sown. Keep a close eye on the areas that seem to be slow to develop; another possibility is that those areas are just a little slower to develop than the others because of a difference in the soil, but they will fill in soon. If a few more weeks go by, there's been sun and rain, and you still have bare spots, you may want to add compost or fertilizer to those areas. The good news here is that if the problem is detected early enough, you can address it and add more seed if needed.

Learning what your meadow plants — like these daisies — look like early in the second spring will prevent unfortunate weeding accidents.

How Many Pollinators Can You Find?

As a new growing season arrives and my meadow begins bursting with color, I look forward to seeing all the different pollinators that may visit during the year (we also get the occasional deer, moose, or black bear, too, but I don't count them!). My daughter, Sadie, and I keep a journal and spend many days waiting patiently to see who might come flying in for a visit. This is a great way to learn about our winged friends and teach myself and the next generation of gardeners how critical pollinators are and the role they play in our ecosystem. We have different categories in our journal, such as Butterflies, Hummingbirds, Bees, and Insects, and we jot down the different species that come to visit. We try to take photos and videos to document as well, just adding to the fun. We'll usually share on social media with other gardening enthusiasts.

WHAT *to* EXPECT
in the FIRST 30 DAYS

At this point, your meadow should be coming in nicely. You should see similar-looking seedlings scattered evenly throughout your meadow. Your plants or plugs should show noticeable signs of growth as their roots settle in and get acclimated to their new growing conditions.

WHAT *to* EXPECT *after* 60 DAYS

By day 60, you should see significant growth in your meadow. If you planted or mixed some annuals from seed into your meadow mix, you may even be noticing the first flowers. If you planted perennial plants or plugs, they, too, may be showing buds or be in bloom. The perennials and biennials you planted from seed will show top growth, while belowground their root structures continue to develop and mature.

This is a great time to identify and pull any unwanted grasses or weeds. If you've planted a large area and you're not willing or able to pull weeds, don't worry too much; most meadow varieties should be able to hold their own against most weeds. If you're not able to identify a weed from a wildflower, don't pull anything just yet and let your meadow continue to develop.

WHAT *to* EXPECT *after* 90 DAYS

Hopefully by now you're enjoying the fruits of your labor. Perennial plants and plugs should be blooming. Perennials that you planted from seed should show lots of green top growth as their roots continue to develop, but probably not a lot of (if any) flowers. Annuals planted from seed should be showing lots of color. Hopefully you're seeing bees, birds, and butterflies visit your garden each day. Your meadow should require very little maintenance at this stage. If you're seeing weeds and grasses at this stage, either pull them or snip the tops off (to prevent them from going to seed).

This is a great time to get to know your flowers. Observe all the different colors, heights, and bloom times of plants throughout the summer. Take lots of pictures and notes. This will help you learn the different bloom times and record the color combinations you prefer.

As the weather cools and the fall season approaches, it's time to think about the second season of your meadow!

CHAPTER 3

Autumn and Beyond

As the cool temperatures of fall set in and your meadow flowers fade, your plants will produce and drop seed for next year's flowers. Following the garden's lead, now is the ideal time to evaluate your meadow and add more seed where it's needed.

Fall is also a great time to try your hand at collecting seeds. You first need to identify the flowers and where the seed is developing. Seeds can take on many shapes and sizes and can develop in pods or nestle in seed heads on the plant. If you've never collected before, start with seeds that are easy to identify and collect, such as lupine, zinnia, or baptisia. You'll need to wait for the seed to mature fully before you begin collecting.

Keep in mind that flowers mature and produce seeds at different times throughout the growing season. If there's a plant you want to collect seed from, note when it flowers, then wait 30 to 45 days from flowering for the seeds to ripen. For most plants, the seed is ready to harvest when the case or pod is brown and dry. Although you may gather lots of seed, not all of it will be viable.

SOWING SEED *for* NEXT YEAR

Fall is a good time to evaluate your meadow and sow additional seed. Maybe your meadow had a bare spot or you want to add more of the annuals you especially liked this year. Your favorite annuals can help fill out the planting, and join the perennials that have already established themselves, in next year's riot of color.

When adding seed in fall, you won't dig up the whole meadow again and prep the soil as you did in spring; you don't want to disturb any perennials that have taken root. Instead, take a hard rake and rough up small pockets in the meadow. This will expose some bare soil for seed sowing while minimizing damage to surrounding growth. Simply sprinkle your seed and press it into the disturbed soil with your foot.

Collecting Seed with Kids

Collecting seed with kids is a fun way to show them where the seed develops on a plant, to appreciate all the different sizes and shapes of seeds and pods, and to engage in creative play (baptisia pods make great rattles!). It's also a chance to teach kids about the importance of the garden for supporting wildlife.

Milkweed is a good example of this. It's critical to the survival of monarch butterflies, which feed on its flowers and whose larvae eat the foliage. Whether you're growing them in your meadow or just hunting for them along the side of the road, it's fun to look for these pickle-shaped seedpods when they burst open in fall, sending their fluffy, seed-laden floss into the air. You can blow into the pods to help spread the seed, or you can pick the pods, bring the seeds indoors to germinate (after a month or so of cold storage in the fridge), then plant the seedlings outside.

My daughter and I keep a journal to identify all the different birds and insects that visit our meadow each year, including which flowers they prefer and which seeds they eat. Monarchs, fritillaries, swallowtails, luna moths, honeybees, and Japanese beetles are just a few of the critters that we're fortunate enough to have visit us each year. Some of these are not exactly welcome (Japanese beetles), but as long as they're not causing major damage, we let them hang around.

Lupine seed pods

Milkweed seed fluff

WHEN *to* MOW

Cutting your meadow back once a year is a good idea to help new growth, and fall is one time to consider mowing. If you decide to add more seed to your meadow (see page 68), cutting back the meadow prior to seeding can make this process a lot easier; removing dead foliage and stems provides better access to ensure good seed-to-soil contact.

If you're not adding seed in fall, I suggest waiting to cut your meadow until the following spring. The stems from this year's growth can provide valuable habitat and food for birds and beneficial insects through the winter months. Just a few short weeks after being cut back in spring, the new growth will be coming on and the cuttings will begin to decompose into the soil.

A brush hog or weed whacker works just fine to cut down the growth. And keep in mind that there's no need to scalp your meadow; it's perfectly fine to cut it back to 4 to 6 inches high. You can also chop up the stems you've cut, so that they break down more quickly.

WHAT ABOUT BURNING?

People ask me whether they should burn their meadow once a year. Burning can be effective in stimulating the growth of some types of native plants and help some kinds of seeds break dormancy. But it can also be very dangerous and is not allowed in some regions of the country or at certain times of the year. It also seems overkill for a very small meadow! Before you burn, check your local ordinances and speak with someone from your local fire station. He or she should also be able to confirm if it's legal in your area to perform a controlled burn.

Rough up the existing soil with a rake or cultivator before sowing fresh seed in the spring.

YOUR MEADOW *in* YEAR TWO *and* BEYOND

As spring arrives, it's time to get excited for another year of meadow magic. If you didn't mow last fall, this would be a good time to knock down the dead stalks and other debris before significant spring growth starts. Cutting now will allow for better sun exposure on the returning plants. You can leave the cuttings right in the meadow, where they will break down and enrich the soil.

Spring is also a good time to revisit the list of plants in your meadow mix, so you can be on the lookout for second-year perennials that might be starting to bloom. Don't get discouraged if a few of your perennials don't flower in the second year. Regardless of whether you planted them from seed, plants, or plugs, some varieties are just slow to develop; some may not flower until their third or fourth year in the meadow. But once they do begin to flower, they should return with flowers for years to come.

If you'd like to see more of your favorite annuals this season, now is the time to sow seed for them (assuming you didn't sow in fall; see page 68). Remember to rough up the soil surface with a hard rake first to ensure good seed-to-soil contact, and to press the seed firmly into the soil to speed up germination.

Cutting back dead stalks in spring will allow the sun to reach perennials growing for their second season.

ONCE YOUR MEADOW
Is ESTABLISHED

Your meadow will continue to evolve as it matures, offering you a chance to play with your plantings. As varieties grow and fill out, you might think about thinning some of them to make room for other plants. You can divide and move plants around your meadow or, even better, share them with friends. You might find yourself adding a new variety or two each year as you learn about different plants. A variety might fade, or a plant just doesn't take; that simply means there's room to try something new!

Gardeners often ask me what kind of maintenance they should do at this point. Here's one of the attractions of this kind of gardening: once a meadow is established, it should require only minimal maintenance — especially if you've chosen the right plants for your growing conditions. Your meadow shouldn't require constant watering or fertilizing or constant weeding.

Rather than worrying about maintenance, consider other ways to enhance your enjoyment of the space. Maybe put out a bird feeder to invite more winged friends, or add a bench or chair so that you can sit and observe the comings and goings in your meadow. Maybe mow a new path through your meadow to add visual definition and provide different access points. These are all things you might include or expand on as the years go by.

Maybe put out a bird feeder to invite more winged friends, or add a bench or chair so that you can sit and observe the comings and goings in your meadow.

75

CHAPTER 4

Meadows with a Purpose

If you have a challenging landscape to work with — such as a sloped hillside, hard-to-reach area, or leach field — a meadow can act as a problem solver for you. Many wildflowers, in particular, adapt to extreme growing conditions and require little maintenance, meaning they'll not only look beautiful but also serve a purpose on your property.

The first step is to determine your purpose, then find the right plants for the job. For example, if you're trying to stabilize soil on a hill, you'll want plants that establish quickly and require little supplemental water once they've grown in. If you're filling a marshy spot, you'll want plants that tolerate a lot of moisture. If you're trying to make your urban plot more nature-friendly, you might want plants that attract pollinators.

Meadow plants can solve all kinds of problems. One spot that's perfect for planting a meadow is over the leach field for a septic system. In addition to adding color and visual interest, the plants soften the look of the area and do a good job of helping a constructed "mound" leach field blend into the surrounding landscape. The reduced mowing is also a benefit. And unlike trees and shrubs, which send their roots farther underground and can infiltrate leach pipes, meadow plants pose no risk to the septic system.

MEADOW PLANTS *for* EROSION CONTROL

Do you have a pesky hill that's a pain to mow each week or one that's losing soil to erosion? Converting it to a meadow might be the answer. With careful soil preparation and plant selection, your hillside can become a place of enjoyment rather than a weekly chore.

It can be challenging to prepare the soil for a hillside planting. Sometimes the area is too steep to till or to break up the soil. You might have to get creative; instead of

trying to prepare the entire area at once, you might divide it up and tackle smaller areas at a time. This can mitigate soil erosion by not exposing the entire slope all at once. If the area is just *too steep* to seed even a little at a time, you may try terracing the area by creating retaining walls using wood, stone, or concrete blocks to prevent water runoff. Another option for an extremely steep slope is to use plugs in the area instead of seed.

Choosing the right plants will play a big part in whether your meadow is successful. When planting on a slope, include a combination of perennials and annuals. Annuals germinate quickly and help keep the weeds down and the soil secured while your perennials are being established. As perennials send their roots deep into the soil, they'll provide long-term stability and erosion control year after year.

Seeding the slope. It's important to account for the slope itself when determining the proper amount of seed for a hillside. I recommend adding 25 to 50 percent more seed when seeding a slope or hill. For example, let's say you have a flat and level 1,000-square-foot area to sow; I might recommend ¼ to ½ pound of meadow mix for this area. If the same 1,000 square feet was sloped, I would recommend 1 full pound of seed. This is to make sure we have enough seed and account for any runoff that you might experience in those first few weeks after seeding. Many times I find that people aren't spreading enough seed to account for the runoff common when planting a slope.

Seeding a slope is one case when I do recommend covering the seed, simply to help hold it on the slope and to prevent the seed washing away. A few bales of straw — not hay, which contains seed — will usually do the trick. Cover the area lightly, so that newly germinated seedlings are able to grow up through it.

Hydroseeding large areas. If you're planting an area that's more than 10,000 square feet, you may want to consider getting a quote for having the meadow hydroseeded by a landscape professional. This can be an affordable, time-saving solution for seeding larger meadows, and the mix of seed and tackifier holds very well on a slope.

Plugs or plants. Another option for establishing a meadow on a slope is to start with plugs or plants, or to use a mix of plants and seed. The plants will set roots quickly and can help with erosion while your seedlings are beginning to grow.

Stabilizing Plants for Hillsides

Wild lupine
Lupinus perennis

Rocky Mountain penstemon
Penstemon strictus

Maltese cross
Lychnis chalcedonica

Shasta daisy
Leucanthemum × superbum

Blazing star or gayfeather
Liatris spicata

Mexican hat or prairie coneflower
Ratibida columnifera

Purple coneflower
Echinacea purpurea

Foxglove
Digitalis purpurea

Black-eyed Susan
Rudbeckia hirta

Plains coreopsis
Coreopsis tinctoria

Blue flax
Linum perenne

Clasping coneflower
Rudbeckia amplexicaulis

MEADOWS WITH A PURPOSE

A HELLSTRIP MEADOW

Okay, so you might be wondering what the heck a hellstrip is. It's that area between the street and a sidewalk that is usually planted with grass or inundated with weeds, and you're never sure if *you* should mow it or if the city takes care of it. Why not replace the grass and weeds with a meadow planting? These meridians or sidewalk planting strips are the perfect spot for some tough meadow plants: they're usually in full sun, have poor soil, and aren't highly maintained.

Once you've confirmed that you're responsible for this area (check with your local department of public works), ask whether there are any height restrictions for plants in the hellstrip. Some towns place restrictions on hellstrips so they don't impede visibility of buildings or roads. Tough plants such as coreopsis, asters, penstemons, and baptisia are good choices. Adding grasses such as little bluestem and blue grama would complement the flowers and add texture.

Tough Plants for the Hellstrip

Common yarrow
Achillea millefolium

Little bluestem
Schizachyrium scoparium

California poppy
Eschscholzia californica

Beardtongue
Penstemon digitalis

Evening primrose
Oenothera species

Deerhorn clarkia
Clarkia pulchella

MEADOWS WITH A PURPOSE

New England Aster
Symphyotrichum novae-angliae

Lavender
Lavandula angustifolia

Sweet alyssum
Lobularia maritima

Gazania
Gazania splendens

Eastern red columbine
Aquilegia canadensis

Blue grama
Bouteloua gracilis

MAKE
MINE MINI

A YARDFUL
of MINI MEADOWS

The Velázquez family was growing tired of their large expanse of lawn in the front yard and wanted to bring a bit of color to the neighborhood. They decided to till up patches to plant with different meadow mixes that would offer a variety of blooms throughout the summer. The neighbors were intrigued by all the activity at first — and very impressed at bloom time!

Before

After

A DROUGHT-TOLERANT MEADOW

Increasingly warmer summers with inconsistent rainfall can make for some very stressful growing conditions for a lot of plants. In recent years, we've seen an increase in drought conditions across the country, from Connecticut to California. As a result, there has been a big increase in demand for drought-tolerant plants in home gardens. A meadow planting of drought-tolerant plants can actually thrive and provide years of color in these less-than-ideal conditions. Just keep in mind that whether you're planting seeds or plants, they'll need watering at the early stages to get them established. All young plants need regular water, especially seedlings, so think about how you will get some water to them in the first few weeks after planting.

Drought-tolerant plants can actually thrive and provide years of color in less-than-ideal conditions.

Drought-Tolerant Meadow Plants

Desert marigold
Baileya multiradiata

Anise hyssop
Agastache foeniculum

Cornflower or bachelor's button
Centaurea cyanus

Partridge pea
Chamaecrista fasciculata

Tidy tips
Layia platyglossa

Oriental poppy
Papaver orientale

Bee balm
Monarda didyma

Purple prairie clover
Dalea purpurea

Bird's foot trefoil
Lotus corniculatus

Sage
Salvia officinalis

None-so-pretty or catchfly
Silene armeria

Sulphur cosmos
Cosmos sulphureus

DEER-RESISTANT MEADOW PLANTS

How can I create a meadow that the deer will not eat? This is certainly one of the top ten questions I've gotten from customers over the past 25 years. So let me be honest and realistic: this can be a difficult task. If the deer are starving, they will eat just about anything to survive; the success of your garden depends on just how hungry the deer are.

Here in Vermont we have lots of deer, but we also have plenty of rural land for them to graze, so they aren't interested in the meadows I've planted. Not far away in New Jersey and Pennsylvania, gardeners also have high deer populations, but they also have high human populations and residential areas have impinged on deer territory. The lack of wild food sources has caused Bambi to become quite a pest in residential gardens.

If you'd like to try a "deerproof" meadow, start by choosing plants that aren't especially appetizing, which includes varieties that are usually fragrant and taste bitter to them. Low-interest plants for deer include asclepias, marjoram, foxglove, monkshood, and catnip. On the following pages, I've included a list of additional plants that will hopefully work for you. Also be sure to pay a visit to your local nursery and ask them for deer-resistant selections for your region.

In some parts of the country, where deer pressure is high, it's difficult to find any plants that are truly deerproof. In many regions, though, deer may find a meadow of zinnias to be unpalatable.

Deer-Resistant Plants

Scarlet sage
Salvia coccinea

Lanceleaf coreopsis
Coreopsis lanceolata

Mealycup sage
Salvia farinacea

Blue pimpernel
Anagallis monelli

Blanketflower
Gaillardia aristata

Wild lupine
Lupinus perennis

MEADOWS WITH A PURPOSE

Common yarrow
Achillea millefolium

Zinnia
Zinnia elegans

Foxglove
Digitalis purpurea

Sweet alyssum
Lobularia maritima

Black-eyed Susan
Rudbeckia hirta

**Red poppy, Shirley poppy,
or corn poppy**
Papaver rhoeas

A BOGGY MEADOW

If you have an area on your landscape with poorly draining soil that collects water — especially in the spring — you may try your hand at planting wildflowers to create a boggy meadow. Typically these boggy spots are found at the bottom of slopes where water collects or in newly cleared wooded areas.

Before you get started, it's important to first survey the area. Is there actual standing water in this area and if so, how often? Most meadow plants won't thrive in constant standing water, so if this is the case with your area, you may want to create drainage to give the water a place to go.

There are plenty of meadow plants that thrive in damp soil. This area of your property may quickly become one of your favorite colorful spots to enjoy throughout the season.

Some plants thrive in spots that tend to be boggy, but not in areas with permanent standing water.

Plants for Damp Sites

98

Cardinal flower
Lobelia cardinalis

Swamp milkweed
Asclepias incarnata

Marsh marigold
Caltha palustris

Rocket larkspur
Delphinium ajacis

Jewelweed
Impatiens capensis

Forget-me-not
Myosotis sylvatica

Giant ironweed
Vernonia gigantea

Globe candytuft
Iberis umbellata

New England aster
Symphyotrichum novae-angliae

Foxglove
Digitalis purpurea

CHAPTER 5

Planting for Pollinators and Wildlife

Many people have become aware of the huge problem facing pollinators — those insects that move pollen from flower to flower, helping to produce most of our food crops. They are disappearing at an alarming rate, which affects not only the natural ecosystem but also our food supply.

The good news is that there is a lot we can all do to help solve the problem. As home gardeners, we can make a big difference by avoiding the use of pesticides, by providing a source of water for insects and birds, and by growing a meadow that's full of plants to attract pollinators and other beneficial insects. Pollinators include many different species of bees, butterflies, moths, flies, beetles, and even bats. Depending on your region, you will see a variety of these pollinators native to your area around your garden.

Planting a combination of annual and perennial flowers allows for early flowers in the first growing season — which pollinators depend on — and provides long-lasting habi-tat that insects can come back to year after year: another key to their survival. Planting a "near-native" landscape (one with both native and nonnative species) usually results in longer bloom time and more nectar and pollen sources throughout the season, which benefits a wider range of pollinators.

PROVIDE HABITAT

To provide habitat for beneficial insects, it's best to leave dead stems and flower heads standing through the winter, then cut them back in early spring. Pollinators need these natural settings in your garden or property to stay protected from predators and to lay their eggs. If you absolutely must mow (perhaps because of homeowners' association rules), consider putting out a nesting box. Nesting areas and boxes are easy to make yourself and provide shelter for bees, butterflies, and hummingbirds.

Plants that are going dormant for the winter offer pollinator habitat, and seed heads provide food for many types of birds.

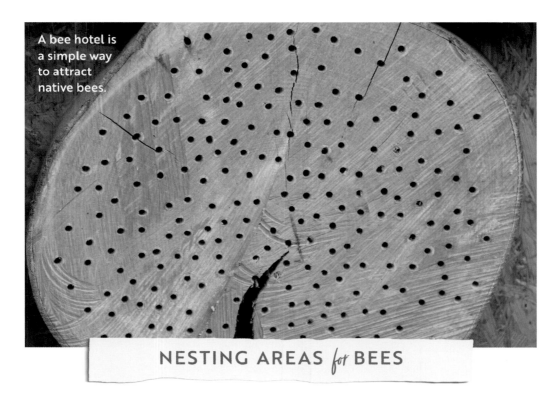

A bee hotel is a simple way to attract native bees.

NESTING AREAS *for* BEES

There are more than 20,000 species of bees, and not all of them nest in the same way. Many native bees nest in the ground and need easy access to bare soil. Come spring, clear away plant debris to expose a 2-square-foot (or smaller) area of bare soil near your garden. This area should get as much sun as possible. If you have space restrictions, you can fill a planter with a mixture of sand and loam to help these native bees nest.

Other native bees nest aboveground. Online, you'll find many intricate examples of "bee hotels" you can build. Though they do add style to the garden, a bee nest doesn't have to be that complicated. Simply take a log, old stump, or block of lumber (that hasn't been pressure treated) and drill ¼- to ⅜-inch holes along one side. The holes should only be about 3 to 5 inches deep and not go through the entire piece of wood. Depending on the size of your stump or log, you can drill anywhere from 50 to 100 holes in one nest. Place your nest at least 3 feet above the ground on a stake, another stump, a fence, or any other secure area. Make sure the side with the holes is facing south and has full morning sun.

NESTING AREAS *for* BUTTERFLIES

Butterflies lay their eggs on the host plant for their species. It's important to provide plenty of nectar-rich meadow plants as well as these host plants in your garden. With a diverse offering of both, butterflies will have a safe spot to lay their eggs, and the caterpillars will have plenty of food when they emerge.

Common Butterflies and Their Host Plants

Try to offer as many host plants in your landscape as possible to help the different species of butterflies in your area. If you have limited space (or growing conditions), milkweed is always a great choice. Even though it only serves as a host plant for monarchs, it provides extremely important nectar for all butterflies and for other pollinators.

Monarch butterfly
Milkweed

Painted lady butterfly
Thistle, hollyhocks, sunflowers

Eastern tiger swallowtail butterfly
Magnolia, mountain ash, willow

Black swallowtail butterfly
Dill, parsley, fennel, carrots

Checkered skipper butterfly
Mallow, hollyhocks

Dogface butterfly
Prairie clover, baptisia

HABITAT *for* HUMMINGBIRDS

Hummingbirds nest high up in trees and shrubs, so you won't be able to build them a nesting area, but you can encourage them to nest on your property by providing them with the materials they need to build their nests:

» Leafy trees and shrubs
» Ornamental grasses
» Plants with soft, fuzzy foliage (like lamb's ears)

» Plants with soft seedpods and fiber (like milkweed, blanketflower, and honeysuckle)

In addition to offering nesting material, be sure to plant plenty of nectar-rich plants for them to feed on! Hummingbirds are most attracted to plants with long, tubular blooms in shades of red, orange, blue, and yellow. Favorite meadow plants include cardinal flower, golden aster, bee balm, and zinnias. Hummingbird feeders help provide these busy birds with plenty of energy and are a great addition to your property.

Citizen Science: Track Your Pollinators

Once you've taken the time to help pollinators in your own garden, you can take your efforts to the next level. Look online at the variety of great citizen science projects that you can be involved with. Many of these track different species of pollinators throughout the country. One of my favorite initiatives is the Million Pollinator Garden Challenge organized by the Pollinator Partnership, an organization with a mission to promote the health of pollinators through conservation, education, and research. The goal of the challenge is to register a million public and private gardens that support pollinators. Once you've planted your pollinator meadow or garden, you can register it on their site (see page 137) and learn all about how you can help raise awareness for their cause.

Milkweed floss provides nesting material for hummingbirds.

Every SMALL SPACE COUNTS!

Even if you're gardening in a tiny plot, such as in a raised bed or on a balcony in the city, you can still do your part to help pollinators by providing just a window box or other container with pollinator-friendly plants like the ones listed below. Pair these easy-to-grow container plants with a hummingbird feeder, some type of water feature (a birdbath is perfect), and a nesting box or nesting supplies, if you have the space. These three elements — food, water, and shelter — can help pollinators in a big way, even in your small space. Here are a few plants you might consider for your small plot:

» Calendula or pot marigold (*Calendula officinalis*)

» Plains coreopsis (*Coreopsis tinctoria*)

» Dwarf cosmos (*Cosmos bipinnatus*)

» Chinese forget-me-not (*Cynoglossum amabile*)

» Baby's breath (*Gypsophila elegans*)

» Dwarf sunflower 'Sunspot' (*Helianthus annuus* 'Sunspot')

» Sweet alyssum (*Lobularia maritima*)

» Dwarf lupine 'Pixie Delight' (*Lupinus hartwegii* 'Pixie Delight')

» Baby blue eyes (*Nemophila menziesii*)

» French marigold (*Tagetes patula*)

» Mexican sunflower (*Tithonia rotundifolia*)

» Zinnia (*Zinnia elegans*)

Calendula

109

Toadflax

Red poppy

Zinnia

Plains coreopsis

ANNUAL WILDFLOWERS *for* POLLINATORS

Annual wildflowers are extremely beneficial to pollinators: they serve as a quick food source for bees, butterflies, and hummingbirds while your perennials continue to develop. Even if your plan is to create a low-maintenance perennial meadow for pollinators, planting some annuals each year — even after your perennials are established — is extremely helpful. Many annual wildflowers, like those on the list below, are extremely nectar-rich, providing essential nutrition for a variety of different pollinators.

» Partridge pea (*Chamaecrista fasciculata*)
» Plains coreopsis (*Coreopsis tinctoria*)
» Rocket larkspur (*Delphinium ajacis*)
» California poppy (*Eschscholzia californica*)

» Toadflax or baby snapdragon (*Linaria maroccana*)
» Arroyo lupine (*Lupinus succulentus*)
» Red poppy, Shirley poppy, or corn poppy (*Papaver rhoeas*)
» Lacy phacelia (*Phacelia tanacetifolia*)
» Zinnia (*Zinnia elegans*)

Lacy phacelia

Quick-Blooming Annual Wildflowers for Pollinators

Borage
Borago officinalis

Calendula or pot marigold
Calendula officinalis

Cosmos
Cosmos bipinnatus

Common sunflower
Helianthus annuus

Crimson clover
Trifolium incarnatum

Meadow foam
Limnanthes douglasii

New England aster

PERENNIAL WILDFLOWERS *for* POLLINATORS

Many perennial wildflowers not only act as a dependable food source for pollinators but also provide shelter and serve as host plants. Additionally, perennials are a great way for gardeners to provide a variety of wildflowers for pollinators and not have to worry about planting each year. Here are a few perennials to plant for the pollinators:

» Common yarrow (*Achillea millefolium*)
» Plains coreopsis (*Coreopsis tinctoria*)
» Blanketflower (*Gaillardia aristata*)
» Wild lupine (*Lupinus perennis*)

» Mexican hat or prairie coneflower (*Ratibida columnifera*)
» New England aster (*Symphyotrichum novae-angliae*)
» Thyme (*Thymus vulgaris*)

Common yarrow

Blanketflower

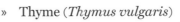
Plains coreopsis

Long-Lasting Perennial
Wildflowers for Pollinators

Butterfly weed
Asclepias tuberosa

Joe-pye weed
Eupatorium maculatum

Purple coneflower
Echinacea purpurea

Wild bergamot
Monarda fistulosa

Anise hyssop
Agastache foeniculum

Blazing star or gayfeather
Liatris spicata

HOST PLANTS *for* POLLINATORS

Host plants play another important function for pollinators: they provide optimal egg-laying sites. One of the most well-known and critical host plants is milkweed (any of a number of species of *Asclepias*), which is the only plant monarch butterflies will deposit their eggs onto. Milkweed and many of these other plants play a key role in helping a wide range of pollinator species, so plant them with abandon:

- » Butterfly weed (*Asclepias tuberosa*)
- » Swamp milkweed (*Asclepias incarnata*)
- » Purple coneflower (*Echinacea purpurea*)
- » Common sunflower (*Helianthus annuus*)
- » Shasta daisy (*Leucanthemum × superbum*)
- » Black-eyed Susan (*Rudbeckia hirta*)
- » New England aster (*Symphyotrichum novae-angliae*)

Easy-to-Grow Host Plants
for Pollinators

Hollyhock
Alcea rosea

Common milkweed
Asclepias syriaca

Indian paintbrush
Castilleja coccinea

Rose mallow or tree mallow
Lavatera trimestris

Nasturtium
Tropaeolum majus

Toadflax or baby snapdragon
Linaria maroccana

Baby blue eyes

Rock cress

PLANTS *to* ATTRACT BENEFICIAL INSECTS

Cosmos

One of my favorite ways to control unwanted insect pests such as aphids, thrips, and mites is to choose plant varieties that attract beneficial bugs to the garden — including lacewings, ladybugs, hoverflies, and parasitic wasps. These insects help keep pest populations in check. Many of the same plants that are attractive to pollinators also attract beneficial insects. Here are a few to consider for your garden:

- » Dill (*Anethum graveolens*)
- » Lanceleaf coreopsis (*Coreopsis lanceolata*)
- » Cosmos (*Cosmos bipinnatus*)
- » Purple prairie clover (*Dalea purpurea*)
- » Siberian wallflower (*Erysimum × marshallii*)

- » California poppy (*Eschscholzia californica*)
- » Globe candytuft (*Iberis umbellata*)
- » Rock cress (*Aubrieta deltoidea*)
- » Wild bergamot (*Monarda fistulosa*)
- » Baby blue eyes (*Nemophila menziesii*)

Dill

Wild bergamot

Easy-to-Grow Plants
to Attract Beneficial Insects

Cilantro
Coriandrum sativum

Shasta daisy
Leucanthemum × superbum

Globe gilia
Gilia capitata

Indian blanket
Gaillardia pulchella

Black-eyed Susan
Rudbeckia hirta

Sweet alyssum
Lobularia maritima

A NATIVE GRASS MEADOW *for* WILDLIFE HABITAT

We've been talking about the different ways meadows can serve a purpose in your landscape, and a native grass meadow provides year-round interest and habitat for local wildlife. One of my favorite winter sights is a native grass meadow dusted in snow. As an added bonus, you'll often spot birds coming to and from your native grass meadow for food and shelter throughout the colder months.

When planning your meadow, consider adding some grasses into the mix along with flowers. No matter what you do, Mother Nature will always toss some unwanted grasses and weeds into your meadow. The more varieties of flowers and grasses that you deliberately include in your meadow mix, the smaller the chance of "unwanted" varieties showing up.

Grasses complement meadow flowers. Their different textures, heights, and colors offer lasting color throughout the growing season, and their seed heads provide food for the birds and offer shelter during winter months. Native grasses are also low maintenance and very adaptable, requiring little water and tolerating poor soils — just like meadow flowers. They have identical traits that make them a nice fit together. Ideally you want to select clump-forming grasses, as they are less aggressive and will thrive well together with your flowers.

Some popular varieties include little bluestem (*Schizachyrium scoparium*), sheep fescue (*Festuca ovina*), sideoats grama (*Bouteloua curtipendula*), and switchgrass (*Panicum virgatum*). These can be purchased in both seed form and as plants or plugs and will adapt nicely whichever way you choose to plant.

If you are going to add grasses into your meadow, the ratio I generally recommend is 25 percent grasses and 75 percent flowers. This usually strikes a nice balance, regardless of the varieties you choose. Of course, you can certainly adjust this depending on your preferences. If you want more flowers, plant more flowers; if you want more grasses, plant a higher ratio of grasses. Whomever you purchase your plants or seeds from should be able to give you some professional advice and make the proper recommendations for your meadow. Below are some common meadow grasses.

- » Broom sedge (*Andropogon virginicus*)
- » Sideoats grama (*Bouteloua curtipendula*)
- » Prairie brome (*Bromus kalmii*)
- » Canada wild rye (*Elymus canadensis*)
- » Virginia wild rye (*Elymus virginicus*)
- » Purpletop (*Tridens flavus*)

Sideoats grama

Plants for a Native Grass Meadow

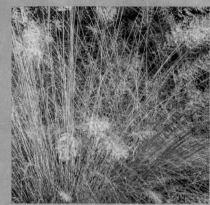

Prairie dropseed
Sporobolus heterolepis

Switchgrass
Panicum virgatum

Northern sea oats
Chasmanthium latifolium

Big bluestem
Andropogon gerardii

Blue grama
Bouteloua gracilis

Little bluestem
Schizachyrium scoparium

122

APPENDIX
Meadow Plants for Specific Regions

When you visit a garden center, you'll notice that many of the plant labels indicate particular growing zones. These are the USDA Hardiness Zones, and they refer to the average annual low temperatures experienced in each region across the United States and Canada. This information can be helpful when you're selecting perennial plants, particularly when taken into consideration with local site conditions (dry or rainy climate, rich or poor soil, etc.) and microclimate (warm or cold pockets on a site or weather patterns in a region that can affect plant hardiness).

I've found that instead of getting bogged down by figuring out growing zones, many people relate better to the concept of growing *region*. Many common meadow plants are hardy across several different zones, anyway: butterfly weed, lupine, purple coneflower, and daisy are all examples of perennial meadow plants that will provide years of lasting color in a wide variety of conditions. So for the sake of simplicity, I've identified six different growing regions and have made recommendations for hardy and easy-to-grow meadow species. These lists represent just a small sampling of the many options available. You'll certainly find more when you begin researching.

NORTHEAST REGION

This region includes: Connecticut, Delaware, Maine, Maryland, Massachusetts, New Hampshire, New Jersey, New York, Pennsylvania, Rhode Island, Vermont, West Virginia, as well as Quebec and the Eastern Provinces. A short growing season with cold winters, unpredictable weather, and four distinct seasons are synonymous with Northeast weather. But don't let that deter you. You can still grow many annual and perennial meadow flowers and some unique ones, too. A meadow can provide big impact with lots of color and maximize the growing season.

» Eastern red columbine (*Aquilegia canadensis*)

» Swamp milkweed (*Asclepias incarnata*)

» Butterfly weed (*Asclepias tuberosa*)

» Calendula or pot marigold (*Calendula officinalis*)

» Cornflower or bachelor's button (*Centaurea cyanus*)

» Partridge pea (*Chamaecrista fasciculata*)

» Lanceleaf coreopsis (*Coreopsis lanceolata*)

» Plains coreopsis (*Coreopsis tinctoria*)

» Larkspur Giant Imperial Mixed (*Consolida ajacis*)

» Cosmos (*Cosmos bipinnatus*)

» Sulphur cosmos (*Cosmos sulphureus*)

» Sweet William (*Dianthus barbatus*)

» Purple coneflower (*Echinacea purpurea*)

» Siberian wallflower (*Erysimum × marshallii*)

» California poppy (*Eschscholzia californica*)

» Spotted joe-pye weed (*Eupatorium maculatum*)

» Blanketflower (*Gaillardia aristata*)

» Indian blanket (*Gaillardia pulchella*)

» Baby's breath (*Gypsophila elegans*)

» Dwarf sunflower 'Sunspot' (*Helianthus annuus* 'Sunspot')

» Oxeye sunflower (*Heliopsis helianthoides*)

» Globe candytuft (*Iberis umbellata*)

» Rose mallow or tree mallow (*Lavatera trimestris*)

Wild lupine

- » Shasta daisy (*Leucanthemum × superbum*)
- » Blazing star or gayfeather (*Liatris spicata*)
- » Scarlet flax (*Linum grandiflorum* var. *rubrum*)
- » Blue flax (*Linum perenne*)
- » Wild lupine (*Lupinus perennis*)
- » Wild bergamot (*Monarda fistulosa*)
- » Baby blue eyes (*Nemophila menziesii*)
- » Love-in-a-mist (*Nigella damascena*)
- » Common evening primrose (*Oenothera biennis*)
- » Red poppy, Shirley poppy, or corn poppy (*Papaver rhoeas*)
- » Beardtongue (*Penstemon digitalis*)
- » Mexican hat or prairie coneflower (*Ratibida columnifera*)
- » Brown-eyed Susan (*Rudbeckia triloba*)
- » Black-eyed Susan (*Rudbeckia hirta*)
- » Sweet coneflower (*Rudbeckia subtomentosa*)
- » None-so-pretty or catchfly (*Silene armeria*)
- » Stiff goldenrod (*Solidago rigida*)
- » New England aster (*Symphyotrichum novae-angliae*)

SOUTHEAST REGION

For the Southeast region, I include the following states and areas: Alabama, Arkansas, Florida, Georgia, Louisiana, Mississippi, North Carolina, South Carolina, Tennessee, eastern Texas, Virginia, and Washington, D.C.

The Southeast region provides hot summer weather and mild winters. Because of its long growing season, you'll want to become familiar with the bloom times for different meadow plants; it's possible to have color for nine months of the year, if planned properly. Because of the hot weather during the summer months, your meadow may actually welcome having a bit of shade.

- » Butterfly weed (*Asclepias tuberosa*)
- » Partridge pea (*Chamaecrista fasciculata*)
- » Lanceleaf coreopsis (*Coreopsis lanceolata*)
- » Plains coreopsis (*Coreopsis tinctoria*)

- » Cosmos (*Cosmos bipinnatus*)
- » Chinese forget-me-not (*Cynoglossum amabile*)
- » Sweet William (*Dianthus barbatus*)
- » Purple coneflower (*Echinacea purpurea*)
- » Rattlesnake master (*Eryngium yuccifolium*)
- » Siberian wallflower (*Erysimum × marshallii*)
- » California poppy (*Eschscholzia californica*)
- » Indian blanket (*Gaillardia pulchella*)
- » Globe gilia (*Gilia capitata*)
- » Baby's breath (*Gypsophila elegans*)
- » Standing cypress (*Ipomopsis rubra*)
- » Rose mallow or tree mallow (*Lavatera trimestris*)
- » Shasta daisy (*Leucanthemum × superbum*)
- » Blazing star or gayfeather (*Liatris spicata*)
- » Scarlet flax (*Linum grandiflorum* var. *rubrum*)
- » Blue flax (Linum perenne)
- » Sweet alyssum (*Lobularia maritima*)
- » Wild lupine (*Lupinus perennis*)
- » Texas bluebonnet (*Lupinus texensis*)
- » Lemon mint (*Monarda citriodora*)
- » Large-flower evening primrose (*Oenothera glazioviana*)
- » Red poppy, Shirley poppy, or corn poppy (*Papaver rhoeas*)
- » Annual phlox (*Phlox drummondii*)
- » Mexican hat or prairie coneflower (*Ratibida columnifera*)
- » Clasping coneflower (*Rudbeckia amplexicaulis*)
- » Black-eyed Susan (*Rudbeckia hirta*)
- » Scarlet sage (*Salvia coccinea*)
- » Ohio spiderwort (*Tradescantia ohiensis*)

MIDWEST REGION

For the Midwest region, I typically include the following states and province: Illinois, Indiana, Iowa, Kansas, Kentucky, Michigan, Minnesota, Missouri, Nebraska, Ohio, Wisconsin, and Ontario. Like the Northeast, the Midwest region has a shorter growing season, but your meadow can still pack a punch of color and lots of variety year after year. By paying attention to frost dates, as well as weather trends and forecasts, you can stretch your growing season and enjoy your meadow as long as possible each season.

- » Eastern red columbine (*Aquilegia canadensis*)
- » Butterfly weed (*Asclepias tuberosa*)
- » Cornflower or bachelor's button (*Centaurea cyanus*)
- » Lanceleaf coreopsis (*Coreopsis lanceolata*)
- » Plains coreopsis (*Coreopsis tinctoria*)
- » Cosmos (*Cosmos bipinnatus*)
- » Sulphur cosmos (*Cosmos sulphureus*)
- » Purple prairie clover (*Dalea purpurea*)
- » Sweet William (*Dianthus barbatus*)
- » Pale purple coneflower (*Echinacea pallida*)
- » Purple coneflower (*Echinacea purpurea*)
- » Rattlesnake master (*Eryngium yuccifolium*)
- » Siberian wallflower (*Erysimum × marshallii*)
- » California poppy (*Eschscholzia californica*)
- » Blanketflower (*Gaillardia aristata*)
- » Indian blanket (*Gaillardia pulchella*)
- » Baby's breath (*Gypsophila elegans*)
- » Common sunflower (*Helianthus annuus*)
- » Oxeye sunflower (*Heliopsis helianthoides*)
- » Globe candytuft (*Iberis umbellata*)
- » Standing cypress (*Ipomopsis rubra*)
- » Shasta daisy (*Leucanthemum × superbum*)
- » Prairie blazing star (*Liatris pycnostachya*)
- » Scarlet flax (*Linum grandiflorum* var. *rubrum*)
- » Wild lupine (*Lupinus perennis*)
- » Prairie aster or tansy-leaf aster (*Machaeranthera tanacetifolia*)
- » Lemon mint (*Monarda citriodora*)
- » Baby blue eyes (*Nemophila menziesii*)
- » Large-flower evening primrose (*Oenothera glazioviana*)
- » Red poppy, Shirley poppy, or corn poppy (*Papaver rhoeas*)
- » Mexican hat or prairie coneflower (*Ratibida columnifera*)
- » Grey-head coneflower (*Ratibida pinnata*)
- » Clasping coneflower (*Rudbeckia amplexicaulis*)
- » Black-eyed Susan (*Rudbeckia hirta*)
- » Brown-eyed Susan (*Rudbeckia triloba*)
- » New England aster (*Symphyotrichum novae-angliae*)

127

Brown-eyed Susan

SOUTHWEST REGION

The Southwest region of the United States typically includes Arizona, southern California, New Mexico, southern Nevada, Oklahoma, and western Texas. This is a region that can present the most diverse weather conditions, depending on where you're located. Dry, hot summers; desert conditions; and cool winters are found in this region. It offers a long growing season, but is prone to drought; you'll need to provide your meadow with supplemental irrigation.

» Desert marigold (*Baileya multiradiata*)

» Cornflower or bachelor's button (*Centaurea cyanus*)

» Farewell-to-spring or godetia (*Clarkia amoena*)

» Elegant clarkia (*Clarkia unguiculata*)

» Chinese houses (*Collinsia heterophylla*)

» Lanceleaf coreopsis (*Coreopsis lanceolata*)

» Plains coreopsis (*Coreopsis tinctoria*)

» Cosmos (*Cosmos bipinnatus*)

» Sulphur cosmos (*Cosmos sulphureus*)

» African daisy (*Dimorphotheca sinuata*)

» Purple coneflower (*Echinacea purpurea*)

» Siberian wallflower (*Erysimum × marshallii*)

» California poppy (*Eschscholzia californica*)

» Mexican gold poppy (*Eschscholzia mexicana*)

» Indian blanket (*Gaillardia pulchella*)

» Bird's eyes (*Gilia tricolor*)

» Crown daisy or garland chrysanthemum (*Glebionis coronarium*)

» Baby's breath (*Gypsophila elegans*)

» Tidy tips (*Layia platyglossa*)

» Oxeye daisy (*Leucanthemum vulgare*)

» Toadflax or baby snapdragon (*Linaria maroccana*)

Blue flax

- » Scarlet flax (*Linum grandiflorum* var. *rubrum*)
- » Blue flax (*Linum perenne*)
- » Arizona lupine (*Lupinus arizonicus*)
- » Arroyo lupine (*Lupinus succulentus*)
- » Prairie aster or tansy-leaf aster (*Machaeranthera tanacetifolia*)
- » Linley's blazing star (*Mentzelia lindleyi*)
- » Five spot (*Nemophila maculata*)
- » Baby blue eyes (*Nemophila menziesii*)
- » Pale evening primrose (*Oenothera pallida*)
- » Showy pink evening primrose (*Oenothera speciosa*)
- » Red poppy, Shirley poppy, or corn poppy (*Papaver rhoeas*)
- » California bluebell (*Phacelia campanularia*)
- » Annual phlox (*Phlox drummondii*)
- » Mexican hat or prairie coneflower (*Ratibida columnifera*)
- » Black-eyed Susan (*Rudbeckia hirta*)
- » None-so-pretty or catchfly (*Silene armeria*)

WESTERN REGION

The Western region includes the following areas and states: Colorado, Idaho, Montana, northern Nevada, North Dakota, eastern Oregon, South Dakota, Utah, eastern Washington, and Wyoming. Spring rains and dry, warm summers can be found throughout this region. Cold winters with frosts and snow provide the perfect growing climate for establishing perennials. Amount of snow and winter temperatures are highly dependent on altitude.

- » Colorado blue columbine (*Aquilegia coerulea*)
- » Cornflower or bachelor's button (*Centaurea cyanus*)
- » Deerhorn clarkia (*Clarkia pulchella*)
- » Elegant clarkia (*Clarkia unguiculata*)
- » Rocky Mountain bee plant (*Cleome serrulata*)
- » Plains coreopsis (*Coreopsis tinctoria*)
- » Cosmos (*Cosmos bipinnatus*)
- » Sulphur cosmos (*Cosmos sulphureus*)
- » Purple prairie clover (*Dalea purpurea*)
- » Sweet William (*Dianthus barbatus*)

- » African daisy (*Dimorphotheca sinuata*)
- » Daisy fleabane (*Erigeron speciosus*)
- » Siberian wallflower (*Erysimum × marshallii*)
- » California poppy (*Eschscholzia californica*)
- » Blanketflower (*Gaillardia aristata*)
- » Indian blanket (*Gaillardia pulchella*)
- » Globe gilia (*Gilia capitata*)
- » Crown daisy or garland chrysanthemum (*Glebionis coronarium*)
- » Baby's breath (*Gypsophila elegans*)
- » Showy goldeneye (*Heliomeris multiflora*)
- » Tidy tips (*Layia platyglossa*)
- » Shasta daisy (*Leucanthemum × superbum*)
- » Mountain phlox (*Linanthus grandiflorus*)
- » Sweet alyssum (*Lobularia maritima*)
- » Arroyo lupine (*Lupinus succulentus*)
- » Prairie aster or tansy-leaf aster (*Machaeranthera tanacetifolia*)
- » Lemon mint (*Monarda citriodora*)
- » Pale evening primrose (*Oenothera pallida*)
- » Red poppy, Shirley poppy, or corn poppy (*Papaver rhoeas*)
- » Rocky Mountain penstemon (*Penstemon strictus*)
- » California bluebell (*Phacelia campanularia*)
- » Mexican hat or prairie coneflower (*Ratibida columnifera*)
- » Black-eyed Susan (*Rudbeckia hirta*)
- » None-so-pretty or catchfly (*Silene armeria*)
- » Smooth aster (*Symphyotrichum laevis*)

PACIFIC NORTHWEST REGION

The Pacific Northwest region can provide a year-round growing climate, depending on where you live. This region includes the following states and province: northern California, western Oregon, western Washington, and British Columbia. Mild winters and warm summers with rain present ideal conditions for your meadows. It's not unusual to have your annuals reseed, thanks to the mild winter conditions.

California poppy

- Common yarrow (*Achillea millefolium*)
- California yarrow (*Achillea millefolium* var. *californica*)
- Wild columbine (*Aquilegia vulgaris*)
- Cornflower or bachelor's button (*Centaurea cyanus*)
- Farewell-to-spring or godetia (*Clarkia amoena*)
- Elegant clarkia (*Clarkia unguiculata*)
- Chinese houses (*Collinsia heterophylla*)
- Lanceleaf coreopsis (*Coreopsis lanceolata*)
- Plains coreopsis (*Coreopsis tinctoria*)
- Rocket larkspur (*Delphinium ajacis*)
- Sweet William (*Dianthus barbatus*)
- Foxglove (*Digitalis purpurea*)
- Siberian wallflower (*Erysimum × marshallii*)
- California poppy (*Eschscholzia californica*)
- Blanketflower (*Gaillardia aristata*)
- Globe gilia (*Gilia capitata*)
- Bird's eyes (*Gilia tricolor*)
- Baby's breath (*Gypsophila elegans*)
- Globe candytuft (*Iberis umbellata*)
- Tidy tips (*Layia platyglossa*)
- Shasta daisy (*Leucanthemum × superbum*)
- Mountain phlox (*Linanthus grandiflorus*)
- Toadflax or baby snapdragon (*Linaria maroccana*)
- Scarlet flax (*Linum grandiflorum* var. *rubrum*)
- Sweet alyssum (*Lobularia maritima*)
- Sicklekeel lupine (*Lupinus albicaulis*)
- Arroyo lupine (*Lupinus succulentus*)
- Russell lupine (*Lupinus × regalis* Russell Group)
- Linley's blazing star (*Mentzelia lindleyi*)
- Five spot (*Nemophila maculata*)
- Baby blue eyes (*Nemophila menziesii*)
- Hooker's evening primrose (*Oenothera elata* subsp. *hookeri*)
- Large-flower evening primrose (*Oenothera glazioviana*)
- Red poppy, Shirley poppy, or corn poppy (*Papaver rhoeas*)
- California bluebell (*Phacelia campanularia*)
- Black-eyed Susan (*Rudbeckia hirta*)
- None-so-pretty or catchfly (*Silene armeria*)

GLOSSARY

ACID SOIL: Soil with a pH below 7.0.

ALKALINE SOIL: Soil with a pH above 7.0.

ANNUAL: A plant that completes its lifecycle in one year or less. It will grow, flower, produce and drop seed, then die.

BIENNIAL: A plant that completes its lifecycle in two years. It will develop green top growth in the first year. It will go dormant, then come back in the second year and flower, produce seed, and then die.

CLUMP FORMING: A plant that grows in small bunches or clumps. These plants are usually not aggressive.

COOL-SEASON GRASSES: These grow during the spring and fall when soil temperatures are cooler, and go dormant during warmer months.

EROSION: The weathering or removal of soil from the action of wind, rain, or other process.

FERTILIZER: A natural or synthetic substance that contains one or more nutrients to help promote plant growth.

GERMINATE: The process of a seed beginning to grow and sprout after emerging from dormancy.

HABITAT: The natural home or environment of a plant, animal, or other living organism.

HERBICIDE: A substance toxic to plants used to kill unwanted plant vegetation. Products such as Round-Up and Weed-Be-Gon are herbicides.

HOA: Home Owners Association. Sometimes they have special rules when it comes to installing and maintaining a meadow.

INVASIVE: A nonnative plant that negatively impacts habitat and ecosystems.

NATIVE: Of indigenous origin or growth. A plant that thrives naturally without human involvement and has been present in a region for many, many years.

NESTING BOX: A man-made structure to encourage and support nesting by birds and insects.

ORGANIC: Of or derived from living organisms; i.e. originating from plants or animals.

PERENNIAL: A plant that continues to grow and flower year after year.

PLUGS: Small plant starts grown in trays or cells, designed to be transplanted into larger containers or directly into the garden.

pH: This is the measure of hydrogen ion concentration indicating the acidity or alkalinity of a solution. Knowing the pH of your soil can be helpful in determining the right plants for your garden, since certain plants grow better in soil with a particular pH range.

SEED STRATIFICATION: The natural process of cold and moisture that can stimulate seed germination.

SUSTAINABLE: The enduring and continuous ability of an ecosystem to thrive and be productive.

WARM-SEASON GRASSES: Grasses that grow during the summer when soil temperatures are warmer and go dormant during fall and winter months.

RESOURCES

Gardens to Visit

I've been fortunate to have traveled across the United States and visited botanic gardens, national parks, Audubon centers, and private gardens from coast to coast. It's a never-ending journey and I continue to be inspired by the different shapes, sizes, textures, and meanings of the meadows and gardens I see. Here are some of my favorites.

The Atlanta Botanical Gardens

www.atlantabg.org

This 30-acre garden located next to Piedmont Park provides a diverse mix of gardens and unique plant collections. The conservation gardens are worth the visit, as is the amazing catwalk/garden canopy that makes it feel like you're walking in the trees.

Denver Botanic Gardens

www.botanicgardens.org

This 23-acre expanse includes more than 50 different types of gardens, from edible gardening to xeriscaping, and they seem to have a new exhibit every couple of months. Their website is also a great resource for gardeners; they are constantly updating and sharing new gardening information.

Lady Bird Johnson Wildflower Center

www.wildflower.org

This national treasure located in Austin, Texas, is a must-visit for any wildflower enthusiast. Founded by former first lady Claudia Alta Johnson and actress Helen Hayes back in 1982, this 279-acre property is the home to over 650 native Texas plant species.

The Los Angeles Arboretum and Botanic Garden

www.arboretum.org

This arboretum features 10 different theme gardens spread over 127 acres, with spectacular waterfalls and enormous diversity in plant species.

New England Wildflower Society Garden in the Woods

www.newenglandwild.org

This 45-acre garden has been a favorite of mine since my first visit back in 1991. Located in Framingham, Massachusetts, it offers a diverse mix of plantings and provides endless ideas and inspiration.

USDA Hardiness Zone Map

To find your USDA Hardiness Zone, go to the USDA website and enter your zip code. https://planthardiness.ars.usda.gov

Seed Sources

The following companies are reliable sources of pure seed, in the quantities needed for establishing a meadow garden.

American Meadows

www.americanmeadows.com
877-309-7333

Beauty Beyond Belief Wildflower Seed

www.bbbseed.com
303-530-1222

Ernst Conservation Seeds

www.ernstseed.com
800-873-3321

Outside Pride

www.outsidepride.com
800-670-4192

Prairie Moon Nursery

www.prairiemoon.com
866-417-8156

Prairie Nursery

www.prairienursery.com
800-476-9453

Reliable Sources of Native Plants

Bluestone Perennials

www.bluestoneperennials.com
800-852-5243

Dropseed Native Plant Nursery
www.dropseednursery.com
502-439-9033

High Country Gardens
www.highcountrygardens.com
800-925-9387

Ion Exchange
https://ionxchange.com
563-535-7231

Minnesota Native Landscapes
https://mnnativelandscapes.com
763-295-0010

North Creek Nurseries
www.northcreeknurseries.com
877-326-7584

For More Information

Growing a Greener World
www.growingagreenerworld.com
470-242-1982

Growing a Greener World is an award-winning TV show appearing on National Public Television that features organic gardening, green living, and farm-to-table food. Each episode focuses on compelling and inspirational people making a positive impact on the planet through gardening and shares DIY information that we can all use at home.

Habitat Network at the Cornell Lab of Ornithology
content.yardmap.org
800-843-2473

Habitat Network is a citizen science project designed to cultivate a richer understanding of wildlife habitat, for both professional scientists and people concerned with their local environments. They collect data by asking individuals across the country to literally draw maps of their backyards, parks, farms, favorite birding locations, schools, and gardens. They connect you with your landscape details and provide tools for you to make better decisions about how to manage landscapes sustainably.

Kids Gardening
https://kidsgardening.org
802-660-4604

KidsGardening has been a leading resource for school and youth gardening since 1982, providing garden grants, research, and curriculum. They create opportunities for kids to learn through the garden, engaging their natural curiosity and wonder by providing inspiration, know-how, networking opportunities, and additional educational resources.

Monarch Watch
www.monarchwatch.org
800-780-9986

Monarch Watch is a nonprofit education, conservation, and research program based at the University of Kansas that focuses on the monarch butterfly, its habitat, and its spectacular fall migration.

National Wildlife Federation

www.nwf.org
800-822-9919

National Wildlife Federation is a voice for wildlife, dedicated to protecting wildlife and habitat and inspiring the future generation of conservationists. Programs such as Butterfly Heroes and Garden for Wildlife are helping to restore habitat and wildlife populations across the United States.

PlantNative

www.plantnative.org
503-248-0104

PlantNative is dedicated to moving native plants and nature-scaping into mainstream landscaping practices. Its goal is to increase public awareness of native plants and related landscaping practices and to increase both the supply of and demand for native plants.

Pollinator Partnership

www.pollinator.org
415-362-1137

The Pollinator Partnership's mission is to promote the health of pollinators, critical to food and ecosystems, through conservation, education, and research. Signature initiatives include the NAPPC (North American Pollinator Protection Campaign), National Pollinator Week, and the Ecoregional Planting Guides.

USDA Natural Resources Conservation Service PLANTS Database

https://plants.sc.egov.vsda.gov

The PLANTS Database provides standardized information about the vascular plants, mosses, liverworts, hornworts, and lichens of the United States and its territories. It includes names, plant symbols, checklists, distributional data, species abstracts, characteristics, images, crop information, automated tools, onward web links, and references.

The Xerces Society

https://xerces.org
855-232-6639

The Xerces Society for Invertebrate Conservation is an international nonprofit organization that protects wildlife through the conservation of invertebrates and their habitats. They take their name from the now extinct Xerces Blue butterfly (*Glaucopsyche xerces*), the first butterfly known to go extinct in North America as a result of human activities.

INDEX

Grow Your Gardening Creativity
with More Books from Storey

by The Xerces Society

When it comes to protecting our pollinators, you can make a difference! These 100 profiles of common flowers, herbs, shrubs, and trees that attract and nourish bees, butterflies, moths, and hummingbirds show you how.

by Michelle Gervais

Before picking up the trowel, pick up the stickers! Layer, arrange, and rearrange your perfect planting using 150 reusable cling stickers with beautiful botanically accurate illustrations, a fold-out design board, and an easy five-step design process.

by Ann Ralph

Grow your own apples, figs, plums, cherries, pears, apricots, and peaches in even the smallest backyard. Expert instruction for pruning a regular fruit tree down to a manageable size will make harvesting a snap.